Liberating Logos

Liberating Logos

Pope Benedict XVI's September Speeches

MARC D. GUERRA

PREFACE BY JAMES V. SCHALL

ST. AUGUSTINE'S PRESS

South Bend, Indiana

ST. AUGUSTINE'S PRESS
www.staugustine.net

Contents

Preface by Marc D. Guerra   xii

Foreword: The "Novelty of Christian Proclamation"
by James V. Schall, s.j.   xii

Liberating Logos

Chapter 1: Meeting with Members of the Government,
Institutions of the Republic, the Diplomatic Corp,
Religious Leaders and Representatives of the World
of Culture; May 25th Hall of the Baabda Presidential
Palace, September 15, 2012   1

Chapter 2: Meeting with Representatives from the
World of Culture; Collège des Bernardins, Paris,
September 12, 2008   9

Chapter 3: Meeting with the Representatives of
Science; Aula Magna of the University of Regensburg,
September 12, 2006   28

Chapter 4: Visit to the Bundestag; Reichstag Building,
Berlin; September 22, 2011   39

Chapter 5: Meeting with the Representatives of British
Society, including the Diplomatic Corps, Politicians,
Academics, and Business Leaders; Westminster Hall –
City of Westminster, September 17, 2010   49

Chapter 6: Ecumenical Meeting; Throne Hall of the Archbishop's House of Prague, September 27, 2009   56

Appendix   60

Biography   67

Preface

Ever since the Prologue to the *Gospel of John*, the concept of *logos* has been at the very center of our Christian faith in God. *Logos* signifies reason, meaning, or even "word"—a meaning, therefore, that is Word, that is relationship, that is creative. The God who is *logos* guarantees the intelligibility of the world, the intelligibility of our existence, the aptitude of reason to know God and the reasonableness of God, even though his understanding infinitely surpasses ours and to us may so often appear to be darkness. The world comes from reason, and this reason is a Person, is love—this is what our biblical faith tells us about God.[1]

Now, the need to escape, to "get out," is also quite prevalent in the West, for ultimately all novelties and thrills are empty, too, when they claim to be all there is. The loss of transcendence evokes the flight into utopia. I am convinced that the destruction of transcendence is actually the mutilation of the man from which all other sicknesses spring. Robbed of his real greatness, he can only resort to illusory hopes. Furthermore, this confirms the narrowing of reason, which is no longer capable of perceiving authentically human concerns as reasonable.[2]

1   Joseph Cardinal Ratzinger, *Introduction to Christianity* (San Francisco: Ignatius Press, 2004) 26.
2   Joseph Ratzinger, *Church, Ecumenism, and Politics: New En-*

It does not take a great deal of intellectual courage or a well-honed moral imagination to recognize that Pope Emeritus Benedict XVI was, quite simply, the most erudite and intellectually impressive man to sit in the Chair of St. Peter in several centuries. An academic theologian by disposition and training, for more than fifty years, he has carefully and consistently brought Catholic wisdom into dialectical engagement with late modernity in a lively and engaging way. Benedict has no doubt been aided in this effort by having witnessed the events that have helped shape the late modern West from the front—surviving the horrors of National Socialism, closely observing the brutality of Communist totalitarianism, experiencing the widespread social and spiritual turmoil of the ideological revolutions of the 1960s, taking part in the *ressourcement* and *aggiornamento* that animated the Second Vatican Council, challenging the voluntarism that fueled the rise of Islamo-Fascism, reflecting on the human import of Globalization, and soberly and firmly addressing the potential De-Christianization of Europe. But Benedict not only witnessed these events, he bore witness to them. Whether it was as a priest or a professor or a Cardinal or the Pope, each time Benedict encountered an ideological "movement" that sought to define the life of late modern human beings, he responded by unflinchingly proclaiming the Good News that God's Eternal *Logos* "became flesh and dwelt among us, full of grace and truth."

That God created a world that is, despite the reality of sin, shot through with *logos* is an ever-present theme in Pope

deavors in Ecclesiology, trans. Michael J. Miller et al. (San Francisco: Ignatius Press, 2008) 199.

Benedict XVI's thought. The understanding of reason that Benedict consistently appeals to (and regularly defends), however, is not grounded in a nominalistic concept or an intellectually useful postulate of "pure" reason. Quite the contrary, it is an understanding of reason that is grounded in the personal *Logos* through Whom God created all things. This same *Logos* took on flesh and liberated fallen human beings from original sin, healing both their clouded intellect and their weakened will. And it is this *Logos* that continues to call human beings into sanctified communion with God in eternal life. Simply put, the reality of the Incarnate *Logos* unmistakably informs every aspect of Benedict's thought.

As the Pope noted in his first encyclical, *Deus caritas est*, Christianity, at its core, unambiguously affirms the reality of human beings' "encounter" with the incarnate *Logos*, with an "event, a person, which gives life a new horizon and a decisive direction."[3] The reality of this encounter, as Benedict repeatedly points out, necessarily expands human beings' natural understanding of the nature, scope, and end of reason. "The ancient world had dimly perceived that man's real food—what truly nourishes him as man—is ultimately *Logos*, eternal wisdom."[4] However, the Christian faith went on to reveal that "this same *Logos* now truly becomes food for us—as love."[5] As Pope Benedict powerfully observes, the liberating "novelty of the New Testament lies not so much in new ideas as in the figure of Christ himself, who gives flesh

3   Pope Benedict XVI, *Deus caritas est*, section 1.
4   *Ibid.*, section 13.
5   *Ibid.*

and blood to those concepts—an unprecedented realism."[6] Indeed, through this unprecedented realism in Christ, it "becomes apparent that truth and love are originally identical; that where they are completely realized they are not two parallel or even opposing realities but one, the one and only absolute."[7]

That modern reason needs to be liberated from the artificial restrictions that are routinely placed on it is a reoccurring theme in the Pope's thought. Again and again, Benedict draws attention to what he calls the modern self-limitation of reason. The exaggerated restraints that doctrines like positivism and reductionism dogmatically impose on the exercise of human reason have, in his view, had undeniably harmful effects on both modern theory and modern practice. Benedict perceptively sees this kind of self-limitation at work in modern ideologies ranging from Communism to Scientism to Constructivism to Historicism. By contrast, the Pope consistently presents himself as a staunch advocate, and eloquent defender, of the genuine liberation of human reason in late modern thought and late modern action. In so doing, he calls into question many of the basic categories and uncritical assumptions that mainline specialists (and practitioners) of biology, philosophy, education, theology, law, and political science today typically accept and routinely employ.

This book brings together six of Pope Benedict's important addresses in one small volume. The themes of these remarkable speeches are wide ranging: he comments on the denaturing effects of Dehellenization, the true grounds of

6   *Ibid.*, section 12.
7   Joseph Cardinal Ratzinger, *Introduction to Christianity*, 148.

religious dialogue, the transpolitical and timeless nature of Christianity's message, the relation of moral and political freedom to truth, the self-limitation of modern reason, and Europe's and the West's enduring Christian roots. Each speech offers an unwavering defense of the splendor and majesty of created human reason's ability to know—and to be liberated by—the uncreated Truth. A source of moral strength and intellectual clarity for a late modern world that increasingly craves both these things, the Pope bracingly challenges modern human beings, Catholic as well as non-Catholic, to be willing to engage the whole breadth of reason. This, Benedict reminds us, "is the programme" with which the enlarged vision of Catholic thought, "grounded in Biblical faith, enters into the debates of our time."[8] The speeches collected in this volume provide a glimpse into the mind and soul of a Pope who remains a man for our season, precisely because he possesses the humility, courage, faith, and charity to be a man out of season. *Liberating Logos* should provide some comfort to those of us who continue to suffer from Benedict withdrawal syndrome.

Marc D. Guerra
Worcester, Massachusetts
May 6, 2014

8   Pope Benedict XVI, "Faith, Reason, and the University: Memories and Reflections," section 62.

Foreword

The "Novelty of Christian Proclamation"

"The deepest layer of human thinking and feeling somehow knows that He (God) must exist, that at the beginning of all things, there must be not irrationality, but creative Reason—not blind choice, but freedom. . . . The novelty of Christian proclamation is that it can now say to all peoples: He has revealed Himself. He personally. And now the way to Him is open. The novelty of Christian proclamation does not consist in a thought, but in a deed; God has revealed Himself. Yet this is no blind deed, but one which is itself Logos, the presence of eternal reason in our flesh."
—Benedict XVI, Paris, September 12, 2008.

"The culture of Europe arose from the encounter between Jerusalem, Athens, and Rome—from the encounter between Israel's monotheism, the philosophical reason of the Greeks, and Roman law. This three-way encounter has shaped the inner identify of Europe. In the awareness of man's responsibility before God and in the acknowledgment of the inviolable dignity of every single human person, it has established criteria of law: it is these criteria that we are called to defend at this moment in our history."
—Benedict XVI, Berlin, September 22, 2011.

I.

Marc Guerra and St. Augustine's Press have brought together in a single volume these six public lectures of Benedict XVI given in Paris, Regensburg, London, Prague,
Beirut, and Berlin. Besides the profundity of matter
treated, this collection represents a singular contribution
to public discourse. Pope Benedict, along with Pope John
Paul II, embodied an extraordinary moment in intellectual
history. Both men were among the greatest minds of their,
or of any other, time. Both were men who were, in their
own right, philosophers and, at the same time, Roman
Pontiffs, occupants of the longest-lasting continuous public office in the history of the world. Both men were not
only aware of the importance of thought, but, also, of its
influence, for good or ill, on ordinary people who seek the
ultimate meaning of human life.

Neither man saw any contradiction in fulfilling these two
separate, but related, understandings of the whole of reality
to which the human mind, at its best, is open. In *Fides et
ratio* and in these lectures, the two popes explained why.
Both of these popes came to the See of Peter with a record
of vast and profound scholarship. Not all popes either have
or need such an erudite background, but it is well that some
do. Catholicism is an intellectual religion in its own right. It
is not based on a myth, but on a fact. It undoubtedly becomes more difficult to conjure up some irreconcilable conflict between reason and revelation when the reigning
pontiffs are leading figures in philosophical and theological
reflection, as well as men of deep personal insight and
human experience.

The lectures and addresses collected in this volume provide a welcome insight into the main lines of Benedict XVI's thinking. Benedict has written some seventy-five books and hundreds and hundreds of scholarly essays—in addition to the many addresses, sermons, letters, and encyclicals he wrote while he occupied the Office of Peter. Benedict's three volume work, *Jesus of Nazareth*, provides a remarkable overview of what revelation is about (and the evidence for and against it). However, the lectures in this volume are of particular significance precisely because they were given in formal, always historical, settings that provided him with an opportunity to range over the history of culture and the origins of human thought as well as the fact that revelation is directed to it.

While Benedict is a very careful and clear thinker, he is also a demanding thinker. Benedict expects, if I might put it this way, "intelligent" readers and listeners. Those who heard these addresses were conscious of the high level of intelligence of the speaker. A sense of hushed awe seems to hover over these lectures. Benedict knows, with Aristotle, that politicians are not necessarily learned or philosophical men and women. But he nonetheless expects them to be intelligent and perceptive human beings who are capable of grasping what is at stake. Benedict, also, knows that politicians are subject to their own pressures, vanities, and desires that often keep them from willing the truth. This realization gave him all the more reason to state the Catholic position in its clearest and most articulate manner, as he does in these speeches, when the opportunity presented itself.

II.

The most important of these speeches, the most wide-ranging and profound, is that formal lecture given in Josef Ratzinger's former academic home, the University of Regensburg in Bavaria. As I have already extensively commented on this lecture, I will here merely touch on its abiding significance.[1] Though this address became famous because of the Muslim protests that followed it, at its heart, the lecture is concerned with the wide-ranging political and intellectual problems that result, in Islam and in the West, when philosophic voluntarism becomes *the* dominant understanding of philosophy and the world subsequently becomes seen through its eyes.

Voluntarism is a recurrent philosophic position that finds at the heart of reality only Will. Whether this will belongs to Allah or to men, it has the same effect: It denies any necessary order in reality. If *what is* really has no order, then, the human mind is incapable of finding anything in the cosmos or man to which it can conform. The logical result of this view is that power, not reason, is left to decide what will be done or left undone. And this power cannot be checked by anything but more power. In the Islamic world and in much of the late modern West, this view, going by various names, is, in fact, the ruling view.

But the main line of the Regensburg Lecture was designed to show the way that revelation is related to reason.

---

1   James V. Schall, *The Regensburg Lecture* (South Bend: St. Augustine's Press, 2007).

Ever since Thomas Hobbes, much of modern thought, especially modern political thought, has denied any rational component to revelation. Revelation is treated as mere fanaticism or folklore. Benedict, however, explains the relationship between philosophy and revelation by pointing out that we find indications already in the Old Testament that God is not a willful arbitrary being already. Especially in *Exodus*, Yahweh is presented under the name "I am, who I am"; in the New Testament, he is presented more simply as "I am." This surprising naming of God provided enormous occasion for philosophic reflection. Indeed, with Augustine and Aquinas, it became the very definition of God as *ipsum esse.*

Benedict understood that the first task of the Christian mission for the Apostles was not, as we might expect, to adherents of other religions, but rather to the philosophers. Thus, when instructed to go to Macedonia, Paul went to Greece. Athens was the home of the philosophers, as Jerusalem was the home of the prophets and Rome was the home of the law. If Christian revelation was not compatible with reason, it could not have a basis upon which it could approach the rest of the world on a recognizable, commonly agreed basis. The intellectual work of the early Christians was to show that reason and revelation are related in a non-contradictory manner. Christian revelation, unlike Islam or Judaism, is not primarily a law code. Rather, it is addressed to reality, to reason, to truth. It was imperative that Christians knew what could be known by reason. For Benedict, the "Hellenization" of Christianity, that is, Christian revelation's relation to philosophy, was itself a first and necessary step in the providence that sent Christians forth to all nations.

The importance of medieval thought lies precisely in its working out the relation of reason and revelation in which both are seen to have their legitimate and proper place. Many philosophers and teachers try to explain what has happened in the world by writing, first, of the classics and, then, moving directly to the modern era—as if medieval thought did not exists. But the New Testament did not think it was necessary to reveal or repeat most of what human beings could know by their own reason. This is why the New Testament is not a political book. The main purpose of theologians and philosophers thus became to show how the two central Christian revelations about God—1) that God is Triune and 2) that the Second Person of the Trinity became Man—are not contradictory or impossible. If these two revelations were actually impossible, then they should be rejected by rational beings. Philosophy, in the very process of working these understandings out, became, as it were, more philosophy. Or, as Benedict himself sometimes put it, revelation was able to "heal" reason.

Benedict understands the main currents of modern philosophy and theology to fall under the rubric of what he calls "dehellenization," the active effort to remove from Christianity any trace of its original relation to philosophy. Effectively, this removal elevates, following a step made first by Duns Scotus and then carried out by modern philosophy, the unbridled will to the central place in human life and the cosmos. As Benedict, also, noted, in Islam, Allah can be understood as pure will, that is, as a being that is not even bound to his own decrees. Consequently, he could will what was evil to be good or what is good to be evil. To claim Allah could not do this would be to limit his power. A similar thing occurs in modern relativism, which denies that there is any reason or natural law to be found in things. It too separates the mind from things. As a result, idealism and subjectivism quickly became the two alternatives to the realism that is based in *what is*.

Benedict's lecture furthermore points out what he calls the "Platonic" element in modern science. Science is based on mathematics, which is, in turn, based in quantity. What science discovers and articulates are, in fact, relationships that are already there. While there are non-realistic logics imaginable, the logic of existing things is found not in the mind but in things and, as such, indicates a non-human origin. Moreover, not all things include quantity in their make-up. These things turn out to be the most important things, the things that must be discovered by other methods of inquiry. To assume that everything is subject to science, as we know it, is to assume that all things are quantifiable. Science, Benedict reminds us, thus has its place, but it is not able to investigate all things that are found in reality. These are the things to which philosophy, at its best, and revelation both necessarily direct themselves.

III.

Another task that Benedict set for himself in these lectures is to explain, patiently and carefully, what Europe is. Europe is not, as he explained to his French audience, simply a combination of Greece, Rome, and modern science. Greece and Rome made it into the modern world through the prism of the Church, and the work, music, and word that Christianity's monastic tradition imprinted on the

European soul. With this mediation in mind, Benedict observes that it "would be a disaster if today's European culture could only conceive freedom as absence of obligation, which would inevitably play into the hands of fanaticism and arbitrariness. Absence of obligation and arbitrariness do not signify freedom, but its destruction." These are remarkable words. They describe the exact direction European thought has gone since it resolved to rid itself of its Christian origins. As we ever more see, this direction ends with the increasing growth of state power shorn of any natural or reasonable check.

The Regensburg lecture stressed the fundamental place of *logos*, word, in the philosophic tradition. At the *Collège des Bernardins*, Benedict remarked that the European philosophic tradition is not merely Greek or European in its depths.

> The God in whom they [the monks] believed was the God of all people, the one, true God, who had revealed himself in the history of Israel and ultimately to his Son, thereby supplying the answer which was of concern to everyone and for which all people, in their innermost hearts, are waiting. The universality of God, and of reason open toward him, is what gave them the motivation—indeed, the obligation—to proclaim the message. They saw their faith as belonging, not to cultural custom that differs from one people to another, but to the domain of truth, which concerns all people equally.

Faith is in the realm, not of custom, but of truth to which mind as mind is, in principle, open.

Out of the monastic tradition also came that combination of word and work that formed the basis of modern science, including economics. Since the world was intelligible and could serve man, he could improve it. Wealth ultimately consists not in things, but in mind working on things. Man, in truth, could not improve the world if he did not know what it was. Nor could he do so if he did not think it worth doing. Europe has a dynamism that seeks something that transcends it. Again, the "deepest layer of human thinking and feelings somehow knows that he [God] must exist, that at the beginning of all things, there must be not irrationality, but creative Reason—not blind chance, but freedom." The world not only reveals an order, it reveals an order that need not have existed, but does.

In Prague, Benedict spoke of the "marginalization of the influence of Christianity upon public life." This theme comes up in the Pope's Westminster Hall address as well. The reduction of Christianity to a purely private and subjective affair is not only a violation of reason, but, also, an exercise of power that would have it solely define what is allowed or not allowed in the public order. "As Europe listens to the story of Christianity," Benedict said in the Throne Hall of the Archbishop's House of Prague, "she hears her own [story]." The roots of Europe "continue."

"Precisely because the Gospel is not an ideology, it does not presume to lock evolving socio-political realities into rigid schemes. Rather, it transcends the vicissitudes of the world and casts new light on the dignity of the human person in every age." The key to Benedict's thought is ever the fact of the Incarnation. What does it mean to mankind as such that the Second Person became man? It means that if

Christ really is the Son of God, if He is truly God and truly man, then, the world ultimately must be different from the way it was prior to His presence in it. The world, at best, can only pretend that the Incarnation did not happen. The persistent effort to deny the Incarnation lies behind almost every heresy. If the Incarnation is true, the world cannot simply be neutral; the world cannot be a creature of its own making.

IV.

In London, the Pope praised the English tradition of Parliament and law. It is, however, interesting that the first person to whom Benedict called to the attention of the English was Thomas More. "The dilemma which faced More in those difficult times, the perennial question of the relationship between what is owed to Caesar and what is owed to God, allows me the opportunity to reflect with you briefly on the proper place of religious belief within the political process." This understanding is properly what political philosophy is about, the politicians' understanding of religion and philosophy. The politician as politician needs to know why both religion and philosophy are needed and present in any public order, why the political order cannot forcefully exclude them. In other words, the politician needs to know that the state that forcefully excludes them is, by definition, tyrannical.

Thus, "what are the requirements that governments may reasonably impose upon citizens, and how far do they extend?" Christianity is not itself a polity. And yet it has a place within any polity precisely because it has something to say and teach to every citizen in every polity, namely, who and what he is, his inner-worldly and transcendent destiny.

The Catholic tradition maintains that the objective norms governing right action are accessible to reason, prescinding from the content of revelation. According to this understanding, the role of religion in political debate is not so much to supply these norms, as they could not be known by non-believers—still less to propose concrete political solutions, which would lie altogether outside the competence of religion—but rather to help purify and shed light upon the application of reason to the discovery of objective moral principles. This 'corrective' role of religion vis-à-vis reason is not always welcomed, though, partly because distorted forms of religion, such as sectarianism and fundamentalism, can be seen to create serious social problems themselves.

Two things are of particular note in this passage. The first is that revelation can "purify" or "correct" reason, that it is not opposed to it. The second is that reason has its own domain or validity. But reason's domain is not so self-enclosed that it cannot be open to truth whatever its source. It is this latter version of truth as self-contained that Benedict often challenges.

In Lebanon, Benedict asks a question that everyone should wonder about: "Why did God choose these lands?" The Pope answers: "To be an example, to bear witness before the world that every man and woman has the possibility of concretely realizing his or her longing for peace and reconciliation." In a sense, it is the constant experience of turmoil and warfare that keeps our longing for peace before our eyes.

A country's wealth, moreover, is "primarily in its inhabitants." We need first to understand the basis of our being. "Our human dignity is inseparable from the sacredness of life as the gift of the Creator. In God's plan, each person is unique and irreplaceable. A person comes into the world in a family." It is no accident that modern "state of nature" narratives of man's origins bypass the family. These narratives characteristically found everything on the individual's will, not his belonging to—and coming from—others. "The destruction of a single human life is a loss for humanity as a whole." Man is thus, as Aristotle said, a political and social being by his nature.

It is in this address that Benedict brings up the meaning of evil in the world. "Evil is not some nameless, impersonal and deterministic force at work in the world. Evil, the devil, works in and through human freedom, through the use of our freedom. It seeks an ally in man. Evil needs man in order to act." However, because this freedom remains, evil can be rejected as well as chosen. "The conversion demanded of us can be exhilarating, since it creates possibilities." Benedict, the pope who is most attentive to music and drama, clearly sees the problematic put into human affairs by this free possibility of choosing good and evil. Likewise, he sees the consequences of choosing either.

Benedict, here again, touches on the issue of dealing with Islam. He is most precise. He knows that dialogue is not possible if words do not mean the same thing, if their aims are different. "Such dialogue is only possible when the parties are conscious of the existence of values which are common to all great cultures because they are rooted in the nature of the human person. This substratum of values expresses man's true humanity. These values are inseparable from the rights of each and every human being." Benedict does not indicate whether he thinks this "substratum" of agreed values and words exists among the various parties. Still, the fact that he brings it up indicates that he understands that this disagreement about basic philosophy is the real problem with any dialogue with Islam.

V.

In Berlin, recalling Machiavelli, the Pope explains that a politician's "criterion and the motivation for his work as a politician must not be success, and certainly not material gain. Politics must be a striving for justice, and hence it has to establish the fundamental preconditions of peace." A politician is himself bound by what he is. He is in the position he is in to fulfill a duty, an office for a good that is not his personal good—except in the sense that a common good is everyone's good. Benedict rejects any image of a politician who is neutral to the basic things of humanity. "To serve right and to fight against the domination of wrong is and remains the fundamental task of the politician." Benedict recognizes that "the majority principle is not enough."

As I noted earlier, Islam and Judaism are primarily religions of law. Their clergy are interpreters of a legal code. Holiness, within each religion, is defined as observance to a legal code. Society is the laws cultural context, and often its enforcement. "Unlike other great religions, Christianity has never proposed a revealed law to the State and to society, that is, a juridical order derived from revelation." Time again, Benedict points out that the origin of Christian thinking on the public order is reason and experience. He takes great care to deal with natural law and how it is rejected by reigning positivist presuppositions. He knows that the view that claims that positive law is the only law in a state necessarily constitutes the reappearance of voluntarism in politics. Here, only what the state legislates and enforces is good and moral; no grounds are acknowledged for resisting what the state proposes.

It is for this reason, in conclusion, that Benedict sees that the state itself must be limited by a higher law. The true meaning of man is not to be found in politics, however useful and necessary politics may be, but in a transcendent order that limits politics and allows for man's freedom to know the truth about his being. "Man too has a nature that he must respect and that cannot be manipulated at will. Man is not merely self-creating freedom. Man does not create himself. He is intellect and will, but he is also nature, and his will is rightly ordered if he respects his nature, listens to it and accepts himself for who he is, as one who did not create himself. In this way, and in no other, is true human freedom fulfilled."

Reading these striking lectures to public officials in leading cities of the world, one is struck by the high level of discourse with which Benedict chooses to address his listeners. He makes it impossible to be superficial, to be ignorant of one's history, of the implications of ideas, and of the centrality of truth as the context of freedom. Each person in each polity has a transcendent origin. Revelation, when directed to us, to our reason, is designed to make us understand that final transcendent destiny to which every person in every polity is ordered. Political kingdoms pass away. But they provide the arena in which the drama of human destiny in its freedom (midst sin and evil as well as grace and reason) is carried out.

The modern state and modern ideology, as Benedict remarked in *Spe Salvi*, seek to replace man's transcendent end with a this-worldly city that can only lead to something far worse than the limited, imperfect states that we actually find in this world. Benedict implicitly tells us that what is, in fact, really wrong in the temporal order is the belief that its citizens are only temporal. This is why he speaks to politicians also, and even primarily, about the Incarnation, about the fact that Europe's real origin is at that crossroads where revelation met reason and law to form one coherent narrative of what we are.

James V. Schall, s.j.
July 2014

Chapter 1
POPE BENEDICT XVI
Meeting with Members of the Government, Institutions of the Republic, the Diplomatic Corp, Religious Leaders and Representatives of the World of Culture

May 25th Hall of the Baabda Presidential Palace
September 15, 2012

Mr. President,
Representatives of the Parliamentary, Governmental,
Institutional and Political Authorities of Lebanon,
Chiefs of Diplomatic Missions,
Your Beatitudes,
Religious Leaders,
Brother Bishops,
Ladies and Gentlemen,
Dear Friends,

سَلامي أعْطيكُم [My peace I give to you] (*Jn* 14:27)! With these words of Christ Jesus, I greet you and I thank you for your presence and your warm welcome. Mr. President, I am grateful to you not only for your cordial words of welcome but also for having allowed this meeting to take place. With you,

I have just planted a cedar of Lebanon, the symbol of your beautiful country. In looking at this sapling, and thinking of the care which it will need in order to grow and stretch forth its majestic branches, I think of this country and its future, the Lebanese people and their hopes, and all the people of this region which seems to endure interminable birth pangs. I have asked God to bless you, to bless Lebanon and all who dwell in these lands which saw the birth of great religions and noble cultures. Why did God choose these lands? Why is their life so turbulent? God chose these lands, I think, to be an example, to bear witness before the world that every man and woman has the possibility of concretely realizing his or her longing for peace and reconciliation! This aspiration is part of God's eternal plan and he has impressed it deep within the human heart. So I would like to speak to you about peace, echoing Jesus' invocation: سَلامِي أُعْطِيكُم [My peace I give to you].

The wealth of any country is found primarily in its inhabitants. The country's future depends on them, individually and collectively, as does its capacity to work for peace. A commitment to peace is possible only in a unified society. Unity, on the other hand, is not the same as uniformity. Social cohesion requires unstinting respect for the dignity of each person and the responsible participation of all in contributing the best of their talents and abilities. The energy needed to build and consolidate peace also demands that we constantly return to the wellsprings of our humanity. Our human dignity is inseparable from the sacredness of life as the gift of the Creator. In God's plan, each person is unique and irreplaceable. A person comes into this world in a family, which is the first locus of humanization, and above all the first school of peace. To build peace, we need to look to the family, supporting it and facilitating its task, and in this way promoting an overall culture of life. The effectiveness of our commitment to peace depends on our understanding of human life. If we want peace, let us defend life! This approach leads us to reject not only war and terrorism, but every assault on innocent human life, on men and women as creatures willed by God. Wherever the truth of human nature is ignored or denied, it becomes impossible t0 respect that *grammar* which is the natural law inscribed in the human heart (cf. *Message for the 2007 World Day of Peace*, 3). The grandeur and the raison d'être of each person are found in God alone. The unconditional acknowledgement of the dignity of every human being, of each one of us, and of the sacredness of human life, is linked to the responsibility which we all have before God. We must combine our efforts, then, to develop a sound vision of man, respectful of the unity and integrity of the human person. Without this, it is impossible to build true peace.

While more evident in countries which are experiencing armed conflict—those wars so full of futility and horror— there are assaults on the integrity and the lives of individuals taking place in other countries too. Unemployment, poverty, corruption, a variety of addictions, exploitation, different forms of trafficking, and terrorism not only cause unacceptable suffering to their victims but also a great impoverishment of human potential. We run the risk of being enslaved by an economic and financial mindset which would subordinate "being" to "having"! The destruction of a single human life is a loss for humanity as a whole. Mankind is one great family for which all of us are responsible. By questioning, directly or indirectly, or even before the law, the inalienable value of each person and the natural foundation of the family, some ideologies undermine the foundations of society. We need to be conscious of these attacks on our efforts to build harmonious *coexistence*. Only effective solidarity can act as an antidote, solidarity that rejects whatever obstructs respect for each human being, solidarity that supports policies and initiatives aimed at bringing peoples together in an honest and just manner. It is heartening to see examples of cooperation and authentic dialogue bearing fruit in new forms of coexistence. A better quality of life and integral development are only possible when wealth and competences are shared in a spirit of respect for the identity of each individual. But this kind of cooperative, serene and animated way of life is impossible without trust in others, whoever they may be. Nowadays, our cultural, social and religious differences should lead us to a new kind of fraternity wherein what rightly unites us is a shared sense of the greatness of each person and the gift which others are to themselves, to those around them and to all humanity. This is the path to peace! This is the commitment demanded of us! This is the approach which ought to guide political and economic decisions at every level and on a global scale!

In order to make possible a future of peace for coming generations, our first task is to educate for peace in order to build a culture of peace. Education, whether it takes place in the family or at school, must be primarily an education in those spiritual values which give the wisdom and traditions of each culture their ultimate meaning and power. The human spirit has an innate yearning for beauty, goodness and truth. This is a reflection of the divine, God's mark on each person! This common aspiration is the basis for a sound and correct notion of morality, which is always centered on the person. Yet men and women can turn towards goodness only of their own free will, for "human dignity requires them to act out of a conscious and free choice, as moved in a personal way from within, and not by their own blind impulses or by exterior constraint" (*Gaudium et Spes*, 17). The goal of education is to guide and support the development of the freedom to make right decisions, which may run counter to widespread opinions, the fashions of the moment, or forms of political and religious ideology. This is the price of building a culture of peace! Evidently, verbal and physical violence must be rejected, for these are always an assault on human dignity, both of the perpetrator and the victim. Emphasizing peacemaking and its positive effect for the common good also creates interest in peace. As history shows, peaceful actions have a significant effect on local, national and international life. Education for peace will form men and women who are generous and upright, attentive to all, especially those most in need. Thoughts of peace, words of peace and acts of peace create an atmosphere of respect, honesty and cordiality, where faults and offenses can be truthfully acknowledged as a means of advancing together on the path of reconciliation. May political and religious leaders reflect on this!

We need to be very conscious that evil is not some nameless, impersonal and deterministic force at work in the world. Evil, the devil, works in and through human freedom, through the use of our freedom. It seeks an ally in man. Evil needs man in order to act. Having broken the first commandment, love of God, it then goes on to distort the second, love of neighbor. Love of neighbor disappears, yielding to falsehood, envy, hatred and death. But it is possible for us not to be overcome by evil but to overcome evil with good (cf. *Rom* 12:21). It is to this conversion of heart that we are called. Without it, all our coveted human "liberations" prove disappointing, for they are curtailed by our human narrowness, harshness, intolerance, favoritism and desire for revenge. A profound transformation of mind and heart is needed to recover a degree of clarity of vision and impartiality, and the profound meaning of the concepts of justice and the common good. A new and freer way of looking at these realities will enable us to evaluate and challenge those human systems which lead to impasses, and to move forward with due care not to repeat past mistakes with their devastating consequences. The conversion demanded of us can also be exhilarating, since it creates possibilities by appealing to the countless resources present in the hearts of all those men and women who desire to live in peace and are prepared to work for peace. True, it is quite demanding: it involves rejecting revenge, acknowledging one's faults, accepting apologies without demanding them, and, not least, forgiveness. Only forgiveness, given and received, can lay lasting foundations for reconciliation and universal peace (cf. *Rom* 12:16b, 18).

Only in this way can there be growth in understanding and harmony between cultures and religions, and in genuine mutual esteem and respect for the rights of all. In Lebanon, Christianity and Islam have lived side by side for centuries. It is not uncommon to see the two religions within the same family. If this is possible within the same family, why should it not be possible at the level of the whole of society? The particular character of the Middle East consists in the centuries-old mix of diverse elements. Admittedly, they have fought one another, sadly that is also true. A pluralistic society can only exist on the basis of mutual respect, the desire to know the other, and continuous dialogue. Such dialogue is only possible when the parties are conscious of the existence of values which are common to all great cultures because they are rooted in the nature of the human person. This substratum of values expresses man's true humanity. These values are inseparable from the rights of each and every human being. By upholding their existence, the different religions make a decisive contribution. It cannot be forgotten that religious freedom is the basic right on which many other rights depend. The freedom to profess and practice one's religion without danger to life and liberty must be possible to everyone. The loss or attenuation of this freedom deprives the person of his or her sacred right to a spiritually integrated life. What nowadays passes for tolerance does not eliminate cases of discrimination, and at times it even reinforces them. Without openness to transcendence, which makes it possible to find answers to their deepest questions about the meaning of life and morally upright conduct, men and women become incapable of acting justly and working for peace. Religious freedom has a social and political dimension which is indispensable for peace! It promotes a harmonious life for individuals and communities by a shared commitment to noble causes and by the pursuit of truth, which does not impose itself by violence but rather "by the force of its own truth" (*Dignitatis Humanae*, 1): the Truth which is in God. A lived faith leads invariably to love. Authentic faith does not lead to death. The peacemaker is humble and just. Thus believers today have an essential role, that of bearing witness to the peace which comes from God and is a gift bestowed on all of us in our personal, family, social, political and economic life (cf. *Mt5:9*; *Heb* 12:14). The failure of upright men and women to act must not permit evil to triumph. It is worse still to do nothing.

These few reflections on peace, society, the dignity of the person, the values of family life, dialogue and solidarity, must not remain a simple statement of ideals. They can and must be lived out. We are in Lebanon, and it is here that they must be lived out. Lebanon is called, now more than ever, to be an example. And so I invite you, politicians, diplomats, religious leaders, men and women of the world of culture, to testify with courage, in season and out of season, wherever you find yourselves, that God wants peace, that God entrusts peace to us. سَلامي أُعْطيكُم [My peace I give to you] (*Jn* 14:27) says Christ! May God bless you! Thank you!

Chapter 2
POPE BENEDICT XVI
Meeting with Representatives from the World of Culture

Collège des Bernardins, Paris
September 12, 2008

Your Eminence,
Madam Minister of Culture,
Mr. Mayor,
Mr. Chancellor of the French Institute,
Dear Friends!

I thank you, Your Eminence, for your kind words. We are gathered in a historic place, built by the spiritual sons of Saint Bernard of Clairvaux, and which your venerable predecessor, the late Cardinal Jean-Marie Lustiger, desired to be a center of dialogue between Christian Wisdom and the cultural, intellectual, and artistic currents of contemporary society. In particular, I greet the Minister of Culture, who is here representing the Government, together with Mr. Giscard d'Estaing and Mr. Jacques Chirac. I likewise greet all the Ministers present, the Representatives of UNESCO, the Mayor of Paris, and all other Authorities in attendance. I do not want to forget my colleagues from the French Institute, who are well aware of my regard for them. I thank the Prince of Broglie for his cordial words. We shall see each other again tomorrow morning. I thank the delegates of the French Islamic community for having accepted the invitation to participate in this meeting: I convey to them by best wishes for the holy season of Ramadan already underway. Of course, I extend warm greetings to the entire, multifaceted world of culture, which you, dear guests, so worthily represent.

I would like to speak with you this evening of the origins of Western theology and the roots of European culture. I began by recalling that the place in which we are gathered is in a certain way emblematic. It is in fact a placed tied to monastic culture, insofar as young monks came to live here in order to learn to understand their vocation more deeply and to be more faithful to their mission. We are in a place that is associated with the culture of monasticism. Does this still have something to say to us today, or are we merely encountering the world of the past? In order to answer this question, we must consider for a moment the nature of Western monasticism itself. What was it about? From the perspective of monasticism's historical influence, we could say that, amid the great cultural upheaval resulting from migrations of peoples and the emerging new political configurations, the monasteries were the places where the treasures of ancient culture survived, and where at the same time a new culture slowly took shape out of the old. But how did it happen? What motivated men to come together to these places? What did they want? How did they live?

First and foremost, it must be frankly admitted straight away that it was not their intention to create a culture nor even to preserve a culture from the past. Their motivation was much more basic. Their goal was: *quaerere Deum*. Amid the confusion of the times, in which nothing seemed permanent, they wanted to do the essential—to make an effort to find what was perennially valid and lasting, life itself. They were searching for God. They wanted to go from the inessential to the essential, to the only truly important and reliable thing there is. It is sometimes said that they were "eschatologically" oriented. But this is not to be understood in a temporal sense, as if they were looking ahead to the end of the world or to their own death, but in an existential sense: they were seeking the definitive behind the provisional. *Quaerere Deum*: because they were Christians, this was not an expedition into a trackless wilderness, a search leading them into total darkness. God himself had provided signposts, indeed he had marked out a path which was theirs to find and to follow. This path was his word, which had been disclosed to men in the books of the sacred Scriptures. Thus, by inner necessity, the search for God demands a culture of the word or—as Jean Leclercq put it: eschatology and grammar are intimately connected with one another in Western monasticism (cf. *L'amour des lettres et le désir de Dieu*). The longing for God, the *désir de Dieu*, includes *amour des lettres*, love of the word, exploration of all its dimensions. Because in the biblical word God comes towards us and we towards him, we must learn to penetrate the secret of language, to understand it in its construction and in the manner of its expression. Thus it is through the search for God that the secular sciences take on their importance, sciences which show us the path towards language. Because the search for God required the culture of the word, it was appropriate that the monastery should have a library, pointing out pathways to the word. It was also appropriate to have a school, in which these pathways could be opened up. Benedict calls the monastery a *dominici servitii schola*. The monastery serves *eruditio*, the formation and education of man—a formation whose ultimate aim is that man should learn how to serve God. But it also includes the formation of reason—education—through which man learns to perceive, in the midst of words, the Word itself.

Yet in order to have a full vision of the culture of the word, which essentially pertains to the search for God, we must take a further step. The Word which opens the path of that search, and is to be identified with this path, is a shared word. True, it pierces every individual to the heart (cf. *Acts*, 2:37). Gregory the Great describes this as a sharp stabbing pain, which tears open our sleeping soul and awakens us, making us attentive to the essential reality, to God (cf. Leclercq, p. 35). But in the process, it also makes us attentive to one another. The word does not lead to a purely individual path of mystical immersion, but to the pilgrim fellowship of faith. And so this word must not only be pondered, but also correctly read. As in the rabbinic schools, so too with the monks, reading by the individual is at the same time a corporate activity. "But if *legere* and *lectio* are used without an explanatory note, then they designate for the most part an activity which, like singing and writing, engages the whole body and the whole spirit," says Jean Leclercq on the subject (*ibid.*, 21).

And once again, a further step is needed. We ourselves are brought into conversation with God by the word of God. The God who speaks in the Bible teaches us how to speak with him ourselves. Particularly in the book of Psalms, he gives us the words with which we can address him, with which we can bring our life, with all its high points and low points, into conversation with him, so that life itself thereby becomes a movement towards him. The psalms also contain frequent instructions about how they should be sung and accompanied by instruments. For prayer that issues from the word of God, speech is not enough: music is required. Two chants from the Christian liturgy come from biblical texts in which they are placed on the lips of angels: the Gloria, which is sung by the angels at the birth of Jesus, and the Sanctus, which according to *Isaiah* 6 is the cry of the seraphim who stand directly before God. Christian worship is therefore an invitation to sing with the angels, and thus to lead the word to its highest destination. Once again, Jean Leclercq says on this subject: "The monks had to find melodies which translate into music the acceptance by redeemed man of the mysteries that he celebrates. The few surviving *capitula* from Cluny thus show the Christological symbols of the individual modes" (cf. *ibid.* p. 229).

For Benedict, the words of the *Psalm: coram angelis psallam Tibi, Domine*—in the presence of the angels, I will sing your praise (cf. 138:1)—are the decisive rule governing the prayer and chant of the monks. What this expresses is the awareness that in communal prayer one is singing in the presence of the entire heavenly court, and is thereby measured according to the very highest standards: that one is praying and singing in such a way as to harmonize with the music of the noble spirits who were considered the originators of the harmony of the cosmos, the music of the spheres. From this perspective one can understand the seriousness of a remark by Saint Bernard of Clairvaux, who used an expression from the Platonic tradition handed down by Augustine, to pass judgment on the poor singing of monks, which for him was evidently very far from being a mishap of only minor importance. He describes the confusion resulting from a poorly executed chant as a falling into the "zone of dissimilarity"—the *regio dissimilitudinis*. Augustine had borrowed this phrase from Platonic philosophy, in order to designate his condition prior to conversion (cf. *Confessions*, VII, 10.16): man, who is created in God's likeness, falls in his god-forsakenness into the "zone of dissimilarity"—into a remoteness from God, in which he no longer reflects him, and so has become dissimilar not only to God, but to himself, to what being human truly is. Bernard is certainly putting it strongly when he uses this phrase, which indicates man's falling away from himself, to describe bad singing by monks. But it shows how seriously he viewed the matter. It shows that the culture of singing is also the culture of being, and that the monks have to pray and sing in a manner commensurate with the grandeur of the word handed down to them, with its claim on true beauty. This intrinsic requirement of speaking with God and singing of him with words he himself has given is what gave rise to the great tradition of Western music. It was not a form of private "creativity," in which the individual leaves a memorial to himself and makes self-representation his essential criterion. Rather it is about vigilantly recognizing with the "ears of the heart" the inner laws of the music of creation, the archetypes of music that the Creator built into his world and into men, and thus discovering music that is worthy of God, and at the same time truly worthy of man, music whose worthiness resounds in purity.

In order to understand to some degree the culture of the word, which developed deep within Western monasticism from the search for God, we need to touch at least briefly on the particular character of the book, or rather books, in which the monks encountered this word. The Bible, considered from a purely historical and literary perspective, is not simply a book, but a collection of literary texts which were redacted over the course of more than a thousand years, and in which the inner unity of the individual books is not immediately apparent. On the contrary, there are visible tensions between them. This is already the case within the Bible of Israel, which we Christians call the Old Testament. It is only rectified when we as Christians link the New Testament writings as, so to speak, a hermeneutical key with the Bible of Israel, and so understand the latter as the journey towards Christ. With good reason, the New Testament generally designates the Bible not as "the Scripture" but as "the Scriptures," which, when taken together, are naturally then regarded as the one word of God to us. But the use of this plural makes it quite clear that the word of God only comes to us through the human word and through human words, that God only speaks to us through the humanity of human agents, through their words and their history. This means again that the divine element in the word and in the words is not self-evident. To say this in a modern way: the unity of the biblical books and the divine character of their words cannot be grasped by purely historical methods. The historical element is seen in the multiplicity and the humanity. From this perspective one can understand the formulation of a medieval couplet that at first sight appears rather disconcerting: *littera gesta docet—quid credas allegoria* . . . (cf. Augustine of Dacia, *Rotulus pugillaris,* I). The letter indicates the facts; what you have to believe is indicated by allegory, that is to say, by Christological and pneumatological exegesis.

We may put it even more simply: Scripture requires exegesis, and it requires the context of the community in which it came to birth and in which it is lived. This is where its unity is to be found, and here too its unifying meaning is opened up. To put it yet another way: there are dimensions of meaning in the word and in words which only come to light within the living community of this history-generating word. Through the growing realization of the different layers of meaning, the word is not devalued, but in fact appears in its full grandeur and dignity. Therefore the Catechism of the Catholic Church can rightly say that Christianity does not simply represent a religion of the book in the classical sense (cf. par. 108). It perceives in the words *the* Word, the *Logos* itself, which spreads its mystery through this multiplicity and the reality of a human history. This particular structure of the Bible issues a constantly new challenge to every generation. It excludes by its nature everything that today is known as fundamentalism. In effect, the word of God can never simply be equated with the letter of the text. To attain to it involves a transcending and a process of understanding, led by the inner movement of the whole and hence it also has to become a process of living. Only within the dynamic unity of the whole are the many books *one* book. The Word of God and his action in the world are revealed only in the word and history of human beings.

The whole drama of this topic is illuminated in the writings of Saint Paul. What is meant by the transcending of the letter and understanding it solely from the perspective of the whole, he forcefully expressed as follows: "The letter kills, but the Spirit gives life" (2 *Cor* 3:6). And he continues:

"Where the Spirit is . . . there is freedom" (cf. *2 Cor* 3:17). But one can only understand the greatness and breadth of this vision of the biblical word if one listens closely to Paul and then discovers that this liberating Spirit has a name, and hence that freedom has an inner criterion: "The Lord is the Spirit. Where the Spirit is . . . there is freedom" (*2 Cor* 3:17). The liberating Spirit is not simply the exegete's own idea, the exegete's own vision. The Spirit is Christ, and Christ is the Lord who shows us the way. With the word of the Spirit and of freedom, a further horizon opens up, but at the same time a clear limit is placed upon arbitrariness and subjectivity, which unequivocally binds both the individual and the community and brings about a new, higher obligation than that of the letter: namely, the obligation of insight and love. This tension between obligation and freedom, which extends far beyond the literary problem of scriptural exegesis, has also determined the thinking and acting of monasticism and has deeply marked Western culture. This tension presents itself anew as a challenge for our own generation as we face two poles: on the one hand, subjective arbitrariness, and on the other, fundamentalist fanaticism. It would be a disaster if today's European culture could only conceive of freedom as absence of obligation, which would inevitably play into the hands of fanaticism and arbitrariness. Absence of obligation and arbitrariness do not signify freedom, but its destruction.

Thus far in our consideration of the "school of God's service," as Benedict describes monasticism, we have examined only its orientation towards the word—towards the "*ora.*" Indeed, this is the starting point that sets the direction for the entire monastic life. But our consideration would remain incomplete if we did not also at least briefly glance at

the second component of monasticism, indicated by the *"lab-
ora."* In the Greek world, manual labor was considered
something for slaves. Only the wise man, the one who is
truly free, devotes himself to the things of the spirit; he views
manual labor as somehow beneath him, and leaves it to people who are not suited to this higher existence in the world
of the spirit. The Jewish tradition was quite different: all the
great rabbis practiced at the same time some form of hand-
craft. Paul, who as a Rabbi and then as a preacher of the
Gospel to the Gentile world was also a tent-maker and
earned his living with the work of his own hands, is no ex-
ception here, but stands within the common tradition of the
rabbinate. Monasticism took up this tradition; manual work
is a constitutive element of Christian monasticism. In
his *Regula,* Saint Benedict does not speak specifically about
schools, although in practice, he presupposes teaching and
learning, as we have seen. However, in one chapter of his
Rule, he does speak explicitly about work (cf. Chap. 48).
And so does Augustine, who dedicated a book of his own to
monastic work. Christians, who thus continued in the tradition previously established by Judaism, must have felt further
vindicated by Jesus's saying in Saint John's Gospel, in defense
of his activity on the Sabbath: "My Father is working still,
and I am working" (5:17). The Graeco-Roman world did
not have a creator God; according to its vision, the highest
divinity could not, as it were, dirty his hands in the business
of creating matter. The "making" of the world was the work
of the Demiurge, a lower deity. The Christian God is different: he, the one, real and only God, is also the Creator. God
is working; he continues working in and on human history.
In Christ, he enters personally into the laborious work of

history. "My Father is working still, and I am working." God himself is the Creator of the world, and creation is not yet finished. God works, *ergázetai*! Thus human work was now seen as a special form of human resemblance to God, as a way in which man can and may share in God's activity as creator of the world. Monasticism involves not only a culture of the word, but also a culture of work, without which the emergence of Europe, its ethos and its influence on the world would be unthinkable. Naturally, this ethos had to include the idea that human work and shaping of history is understood as sharing in the work of the Creator, and must be evaluated in those terms. Where such evaluation is lacking, where man arrogates to himself the status of god-like creator, his shaping of the world can quickly turn into destruction of the world.

We set out from the premise that the basic attitude of monks in the face of the collapse of the old order and its certainties was *quaerere Deum*—setting out in search of God. We could describe this as the truly philosophical attitude: looking beyond the penultimate, and setting out in search of the ultimate and the true. By becoming a monk, a man set out on a broad and noble path, but he had already found the direction he needed: the word of the Bible, in which he heard God himself speaking. Now he had to try to understand him, so as to be able to approach him. So the monastic journey is indeed a journey into the inner world of the received word, even if an infinite distance is involved. Within the monks' seeking there is already contained, in some respects, a finding. Therefore, if such seeking is to be possible at all, there has to be an initial spur, which not only arouses the will to seek, but also makes it possible to believe that the way is concealed within this word, or rather: that in this word, God himself has set out towards men, and hence men can come to God through it. To put it another way: there must be proclamation, which speaks to man and so creates conviction, which in turn can become life. If a way is to be opened up into the heart of the biblical word as God's word, this word must first of all be proclaimed outwardly. The classic formulation of the Christian faith's intrinsic need to make itself communicable to others, is a phrase from the *First Letter of Peter*, which in medieval theology was regarded as the biblical basis for the work of theologians: "Always have your answer ready for people who ask you the reason (the *logos*) for the hope that you all have" (3:15). (The *Logos*, the reason for hope must become *apo-logía;* it must become a response.) In fact, Christians of the nascent Church did not regard their missionary proclamation as propaganda, designed to enlarge their particular group, but as an inner necessity, consequent upon the nature of their faith: the God in whom they believed was the God of all people, the one, true God, who had revealed himself in the history of Israel and ultimately in his Son, thereby supplying the answer which was of concern to everyone and for which all people, in their innermost hearts, are waiting. The universality of God, and of reason open towards him, is what gave them the motivation—indeed, the obligation—to proclaim the message. They saw their faith as belonging, not to cultural custom that differs from one people to another, but to the domain of truth, which concerns all people equally.

The fundamental structure of Christian proclamation "outwards"—towards searching and questioning mankind—is seen in Saint Paul's address at the Areopagus.

We should remember that the Areopagus was not a form of academy at which the most illustrious minds would meet for discussion of lofty matters, but a court of justice, which was competent in matters of religion and ought to have opposed the import of foreign religions. This is exactly what Paul is reproached for: "he seems to be a preacher of foreign divinities" (*Acts* 17:18). To this, Paul responds: "I have found an altar of yours with this inscription: 'to an unknown god.' What therefore you worship as unknown, this I proclaim to you" (17:23). Paul is not proclaiming unknown gods. He is proclaiming him whom men do not know and yet do know—the unknown-known; the one they are seeking, whom ultimately they know already, and who yet remains the unknown and unrecognizable. The deepest layer of human thinking and feeling somehow knows that he must exist, that at the beginning of all things, there must be not irrationality, but creative Reason—not blind chance, but freedom. Yet even though all men somehow know this, as Paul expressly says in the *Letter to the Romans* (1:21), this knowledge remains unreal: a God who is merely imagined and invented is not God at all. If he does not reveal himself, we cannot gain access to him. The novelty of Christian proclamation is that it can now say to all peoples: he has revealed himself. He personally. And now the way to him is open. The novelty of Christian proclamation does not consist in a thought, but in a deed: God has revealed himself. Yet this is no blind deed, but one which is itself *Logos*—the presence of eternal reason in our flesh. *Verbum caro factum est* (*Jn.* 1:14): just so, amid what is made (*factum*) there is now *Logos, Logos* is among us. Creation (*factum*) is rational. Naturally, the humility of reason is always needed, in order to accept it: man's humility, which responds to God's humility.

Our present situation differs in many respects from the one that Paul encountered in Athens, yet despite the difference, the two situations also have much in common. Our cities are no longer filled with altars and with images of multiple deities. God has truly become for many the great unknown. But just as in the past, when behind the many images of God the question concerning the unknown God was hidden and present, so too the present absence of God is silently besieged by the question concerning him. *Quaerere Deum*—to seek God and to let oneself be found by him, that is today no less necessary than in former times. A purely positivistic culture which tried to drive the question concerning God into the subjective realm, as being unscientific, would be the capitulation of reason, the renunciation of its highest possibilities, and hence a disaster for humanity, with very grave consequences. What gave Europe's culture its foundation— the search for God and the readiness to listen to him—remains today the basis of any genuine culture. Thank you.

Chapter 3
POPE BENEDICT XVI
Meeting with the
Representatives of Science

Aula Magna of the University of Regensburg
September 12, 2006

"Faith, Reason and the University
Memories and Reflections"

Your Eminences, Your Magnificences, Your Excellencies,
Distinguished Ladies and Gentlemen,

It is a moving experience for me to be back again in the university and to be able once again to give a lecture at this podium. I think back to those years when, after a pleasant period at the Freisinger Hochschule, I began teaching at the University of Bonn. That was in 1959, in the days of the old university made up of ordinary professors. The various chairs had neither assistants nor secretaries, but in recompense there was much direct contact with students and in particular among the professors themselves. We would meet before and after lessons in the rooms of the teaching staff. There was a lively exchange with historians, philosophers, philologists and, naturally, between the two theological faculties. Once a semester there was a *dies academicus*, when professors from every faculty appeared before the students of the entire university, making possible a genuine experience of *universitas*—something that you too, Magnificent Rector, just mentioned—the experience, in other words, of the fact that despite our specializations which at times make it difficult to communicate with each other, we made up a whole, working in everything on the basis of a single rationality with its various aspects and sharing responsibility for the right use of reason— this reality became a lived experience. The university was also very proud of its two theological faculties. It was clear that, by inquiring about the reasonableness of faith, they too carried out a work which is necessarily part of the "whole" of the *universitas scientiarum*, even if not everyone could share the faith which theologians seek to correlate with reason as a whole. This profound sense of coherence within the universe of reason was not troubled, even when it was once reported that a colleague had said there was something odd about our university: it had two faculties devoted to something that did not exist: God. That even in the face of such radical skepticism it is still necessary and reasonable to raise the question of God through the use of reason, and to do so in the context of the tradition of the Christian faith: this, within the university as a whole, was accepted without question.

I was reminded of all this recently, when I read the edition by Professor Theodore Khoury (Münster) of part of the dialogue carried on—perhaps in 1391 in the winter barracks near Ankara—by the erudite Byzantine emperor Manuel II Paleologus and an educated Persian on the subject of Christianity and Islam, and the truth of both.[1] It was presumably the

1   Of the total number of 26 conversations (διάλεξις– Khoury translates this as "controversy") in the dialogue ("Entretien"),

emperor himself who set down this dialogue, during the siege of Constantinople between 1394 and 1402; and this would explain why his arguments are given in greater detail than those of his Persian interlocutor.[2] The dialogue ranges widely over the structures of faith contained in the Bible and in the Qur'an, and deals especially with the image of God and of man, while necessarily returning repeatedly to the relationship between— as they were called—three "Laws" or "rules of life": the Old Testament, the New Testament and the Qur'an. It is not my intention to discuss this question in the present lecture; here I would like to discuss only one point—itself rather marginal to the dialogue as a whole–which, in the context of the issue of "faith and reason," I found interesting and which can serve as the starting-point for my reflections on this issue.

In the seventh conversation (διάλεξις – that surah 2, 256 reads: "There is no compulsion in religion."

T. Khoury published the 7th tradition and on the structure of the dialogue, together with brief summaries of the "controversies" not included in the edition; the Greek text is accompanied by a French translation: "Manuel II Paléologue, Entretiens avec un Musulman. 7ᵉ Controverse," *Sources Chrétiennes* n. 115, Paris 1966. In the meantime, Karl Förstel published in *Corpus Islamico-Christianum* (*Series Graeca* ed. A. T. Khoury and R. Glei) an edition of the text in Greek and German with commentary: "Manuel II. Paleologus, Dialoge mit einem Muslim," 3 vols., Würzburg-Altenberge 1993–1996. As early as 1966, E. Trapp had published the Greek text with an introduction as vol. II of *Wiener byzantinische Studien*. I shall be quoting from Khoury's edition.

2 On the origin and redaction of the dialogue, cf. Khoury, pp. 22–29; extensive comments in this regard can also be found in the editions of Förstel and Trapp.

According to some of the experts, this is probably one of the *suras* of the early period, when Mohammed was still powerless and under threat. But naturally the emperor also knew the instructions, developed later and recorded in the Qur'an, concerning holy war. Without descending to details, such as the difference in treatment accorded to those who have the "Book" and the "infidels," he addresses his interlocutor with a startling brusqueness, a brusqueness that we find unacceptable, on the central question about the relationship between religion and violence in general, saying: "Show me just what Mohammed brought that was new, and there you will find things only evil and inhuman, such as his command to spread by the sword the faith he preached."[3] re of God and the nature of the soul. "God," he says, "is not pleased by blood—and not acting reasonably (συ 'νλόγω) is contrary to God's nature. Faith is born of the soul, not the body. Whoever would lead someone to faith needs the ability to speak well and to reason properly, without violence and threats. . . . To convince a reasonable soul, one does not need a strong arm, or weapons of any

3   Controversy VII, 2 c: Khoury, pp. 142–43; Förstel, vol. I, VII. Dialog 1.5, pp. 240–41. In the Muslim world, this quotation has unfortunately been taken as an expression of my personal position, thus arousing understandable indignation. I hope that the reader of my text can see immediately that this sentence does not express my personal view of the Qur'an, for which I have the respect due to the holy book of a great religion. In quoting the text of the Emperor Manuel II, I intended solely to draw out the essential relationship between faith and reason. On this point I am in agreement with Manuel II, but without endorsing his polemic.

kind, or any other means of threatening a person with death."[4]

The decisive statement in this argument against violent conversion is this: not to act in accordance with reason is contrary to God's nature.[5] The editor, Theodore Khoury, observes: For the emperor, as a Byzantine shaped by Greek philosophy, this statement is self-evident. But for Muslim teaching, God is absolutely transcendent. His will is not bound up with any of our categories, even that of rationality.[6] Here Khoury quotes a work of the noted French Islamist R. Arnaldez, who points out that Ibn Hazm went so far as to state that God is not bound even by his own word, and that nothing would oblige him to reveal the truth to us. Were it God's will, we would even have to practice idolatry.[7]

At this point, as far as understanding of God and thus the concrete practice of religion is concerned, we are faced with an unavoidable dilemma. Is the conviction that acting unreasonably contradicts God's nature merely a Greek idea, or is it always and intrinsically true? I believe that here we can see the profound harmony between what is Greek in the best sense of the word and the biblical understanding of faith

4   Controversy VII, 3 b–c: Khoury, pp. 144–45; Förstel vol. I, VII. Dialog 1.6, pp. 240–43.
5   It was purely for the sake of this statement that I quoted the dialogue between Manuel and his Persian interlocutor. In this statement the theme of my subsequent reflections emerges.
6   Cf. Khoury, p. 144, n. 1.
7   R. Arnaldez, *Grammaire et théologie chez Ibn Hazm de Cordoue*, Paris 1956, p. 13; cf. Khoury, p. 144. The fact that comparable positions exist in the theology of the late Middle Ages will appear later in my discourse.

in God. Modifying the first verse of the Book of Genesis, the first verse of the whole Bible, John began the prologue of his Gospel with the words: "In the beginning was the λόγος." This is the very word used by the emperor: God acts, σὺ 'υλο-'γω, with *logos. Logos* means both reason and word—a reason which is creative and capable of self-communication, precisely as reason. John thus spoke the final word on the biblical concept of God, and in this word all the often toilsome and tortuous threads of biblical faith find their culmination and synthesis. In the beginning was the *logos*, and the *logos* is God, says the Evangelist. The encounter between the biblical message and Greek thought did not happen by chance. The vision of Saint Paul, who saw the roads to Asia barred and in a dream saw a Macedonian man plead with him: "Come over to Macedonia and help us!" (cf. *Acts* 16:6-10)—this vision can be interpreted as a "distillation" of the intrinsic necessity of a rapprochement between biblical faith and Greek inquiry.

In point of fact, this rapprochement had been going on for some time. The mysterious name of God, revealed from the burning bush, a name which separates this God from all other divinities with their many names and simply asserts being, "I am," already presents a challenge to the notion of myth, to which Socrates' attempt to vanquish and transcend myth stands in close analogy.[8] Within the Old Testament,

8   Regarding the widely discussed interpretation of the episode of the burning bush, I refer to my book *Introduction to Christianity,* London 1969, pp. 77–93 (originally published in German as *Einführung in das Christentum,* Munich 1968; N.B. the pages quoted refer to the entire chapter entitled "The Biblical Belief in God"). I think that my statements in that book,

the process which started at the burning bush came to new maturity at the time of the Exile, when the God of Israel, an Israel now deprived of its land and worship, was proclaimed as the God of heaven and earth and described in a simple formula which echoes the words uttered at the burning bush: "I am." This new understanding of God is accompanied by a kind of enlightenment, which finds stark expression in the mockery of gods who are merely the work of human hands (cf. *Ps* 115). Thus, despite the bitter conflict with those Hellenistic rulers who sought to accommodate it forcibly to the customs and idolatrous cult of the Greeks, biblical faith, in the Hellenistic period, encountered the best of Greek thought at a deep level, resulting in a mutual enrichment evident especially in the later wisdom literature. Today we know that the Greek translation of the Old Testament produced at Alexandria—the Septuagint—is more than a simple (and in that sense really less than satisfactory) translation of the Hebrew text: it is an independent textual witness and a distinct and important step in the history of revelation, one which brought about this encounter in a way that was decisive for the birth and spread of Christianity.[9] A profound encounter of faith and reason is taking place here, an encounter between genuine enlightenment and religion. From the very heart of Christian faith and, at the same time, the heart of Greek thought now joined to faith, Manuel II

despite later developments in the discussion, remain valid today.

9   Cf. A. Schenker, "L'Écriture sainte subsiste en plusieurs formes canoniques simultanées," in *L'Interpretazione della Bibbia nella Chiesa. Atti del Simposio promosso dalla Congregazione per la Dottrina della Fede*, Vatican City 2001, pp. 178–86.

was able to say: Not to act "with *logos*" is contrary to God's nature.

In all honesty, one must observe that in the late Middle Ages we find trends in theology which would sunder this synthesis between the Greek spirit and the Christian spirit. In contrast with the so-called intellectualism of Augustine and Thomas, there arose with Duns Scotus a voluntarism which, in its later developments, led to the claim that we can only know God's *voluntas ordinata*. Beyond this is the realm of God's freedom, in virtue of which he could have done the opposite of everything he has actually done. This gives rise to positions which clearly approach those of Ibn Hazm and might even lead to the image of a capricious God, who is not even bound to truth and goodness. God's transcendence and otherness are so exalted that our reason, our sense of the true and good, are no longer an authentic mirror of God, whose deepest possibilities remain eternally unattainable and hidden behind his actual decisions. As opposed to this, the faith of the Church has always insisted that between God and us, between his eternal Creator Spirit and our created reason there exists a real analogy, in which—as the Fourth Lateran Council in 1215 stated—unlikeness remains infinitely greater than likeness, yet not to the point of abolishing analogy and its language. God does not become more divine when we push him away from us in a sheer, impenetrable voluntarism; rather, the truly divine God is the God who has revealed himself as *logos* and, as *logos*, has acted and continues to act lovingly on our behalf. Certainly, love, as Saint Paul says, "transcends" knowledge and is thereby capable of perceiving more than thought alone (cf. *Eph* 3:19); nonetheless it continues to be love of the God who is *Logos*. Consequently,

Christian worship is, again to quote Paul – "λογικη λατρεία," worship in harmony with the eternal Word and with our reason (cf. *Rom* 12:1).[10]

This inner rapprochement between biblical faith and Greek philosophical inquiry was an event of decisive importance not only from the standpoint of the history of religions, but also from that of world history—it is an event which concerns us even today. Given this convergence, it is not surprising that Christianity, despite its origins and some significant developments in the East, finally took on its historically decisive character in Europe. We can also express this the other way around: this convergence, with the subsequent addition of the Roman heritage, created Europe and remains the foundation of what can rightly be called Europe.

The thesis that the critically purified Greek heritage forms an integral part of Christian faith has been countered by the call for a dehellenization of Christianity—a call which has more and more dominated theological discussions since the beginning of the modern age. Viewed more closely, three stages can be observed in the program of dehellenization: although interconnected, they are clearly distinct from one another in their motivations and objectives.[11]

10 On this matter I expressed myself in greater detail in my book *The Spirit of the Liturgy*, San Francisco 2000, pp. 44–50.

11 Of the vast literature on the theme of dehellenization, I would like to mention above all: A. Grillmeier, "Hellenisierung-Judaisierung des Christentums als Deuteprinzipien der Geschichte des kirchlichen Dogmas," in idem, *Mit ihm und in ihm. Christologische Forschungen und Perspektiven*, Freiburg 1975, pp. 423–88.

Dehellenization first emerges in connection with the postulates of the Reformation in the sixteenth century. Looking at the tradition of scholastic theology, the Reformers thought they were confronted with a faith system totally conditioned by philosophy, that is to say an articulation of the faith based on an alien system of thought. As a result, faith no longer appeared as a living historical Word but as one element of an overarching philosophical system. The principle of *sola scriptura*, on the other hand, sought faith in its pure, primordial form, as originally found in the biblical Word. Metaphysics appeared as a premise derived from another source, from which faith had to be liberated in order to become once more fully itself. When Kant stated that he needed to set thinking aside in order to make room for faith, he carried this program forward with a radicalism that the Reformers could never have foreseen. He thus anchored faith exclusively in practical reason, denying it access to reality as a whole.

The liberal theology of the nineteenth and twentieth centuries ushered in a second stage in the process of dehellenization, with Adolf von Harnack as its outstanding representative. When I was a student, and in the early years of my teaching, this program was highly influential in Catholic theology too. It took as its point of departure Pascal's distinction between the God of the philosophers and the God of Abraham, Isaac and Jacob. In my inaugural lecture at Bonn in 1959, I tried to address the issue,[12] and I do not

12 Newly published with commentary by Heino Sonnemans (ed.): *Joseph Ratzinger-Benedikt XVI, Der Gott des Glaubens und der Gott der Philosophien. Ein Beitrag zum Problem der the-*

intend to repeat here what I said on that occasion, but I would like to describe at least briefly what was new about this second stage of dehellenization. Harnack's central idea was to return simply to the man Jesus and to his simple message, underneath the accretions of theology and indeed of hellenization: this simple message was seen as the culmination of the religious development of humanity. Jesus was said to have put an end to worship in favor of morality. In the end he was presented as the father of a humanitarian moral message. Fundamentally, Harnack's goal was to bring Christianity back into harmony with modern reason, liberating it, that is to say, from seemingly philosophical and theological elements, such as faith in Christ's divinity and the triune God. In this sense, historical-critical exegesis of the New Testament, as he saw it, restored to theology its place within the university: theology, for Harnack, is something essentially historical and therefore strictly scientific. What it is able to say critically about Jesus is, so to speak, an expression of practical reason and consequently it can take its rightful place within the university. Behind this thinking lies the modern self-limitation of reason, classically expressed in Kant's "Critiques," but in the meantime further radicalized by the impact of the natural sciences. This modern concept of reason is based, to put it briefly, on a synthesis between Platonism (Cartesianism) and empiricism, a synthesis confirmed by the success of technology. On the one hand it presupposes the mathematical structure of matter, its intrinsic rationality, which makes it possible to understand how matter works and use it efficiently: this basic premise is, so to speak, the Platonic element in the modern understanding of nature. On the other hand, there is nature's capacity to be exploited for our purposes, and here only the possibility of verification or falsification through experimentation can yield decisive certainty. The weight between the two poles can, depending on the circumstances, shift from one side to the other. As strongly positivistic a thinker as J. Monod has declared himself a convinced Platonist/Cartesian.

This gives rise to two principles which are crucial for the issue we have raised. First, only the kind of certainty resulting from the interplay of mathematical and empirical elements can be considered scientific. Anything that would claim to be science must be measured against this criterion. Hence the human sciences, such as history, psychology, sociology and philosophy, attempt to conform themselves to this canon of scientificity. A second point, which is important for our reflections, is that by its very nature this method excludes the question of God, making it appear an unscientific or pre-scientific question. Consequently, we are faced with a reduction of the radius of science and reason, one which needs to be questioned.

I will return to this problem later. In the meantime, it must be observed that from this standpoint any attempt to maintain theology's claim to be "scientific" would end up reducing Christianity to a mere fragment of its former self. But we must say more: if science as a whole is this and this alone, then it is man himself who ends up being reduced, for the specifically human questions about our origin and destiny, the questions raised by religion and ethics, then have no place within the purview of collective reason as defined by "science," so understood, and must thus be relegated to the realm of the subjective. The subject then decides, on the basis of his experiences, what he considers tenable in matters of religion, and the subjective "conscience" becomes the sole arbiter of what is ethical. In this way, though, ethics and religion lose their power to create a community and become a completely personal matter. This is a dangerous state of affairs for humanity, as we see from the disturbing pathologies of religion and reason which necessarily erupt when reason is so reduced that questions of religion and ethics no longer concern it. Attempts to construct an ethic from the rules of evolution or from psychology and sociology, end up being simply inadequate.

Before I draw the conclusions to which all this has been leading, I must briefly refer to the third stage of dehellenization, which is now in progress. In the light of our experience with cultural pluralism, it is often said nowadays that the synthesis with Hellenism achieved in the early Church was an initial enculturation which ought not to be binding on other cultures. The latter are said to have the right to return to the simple message of the New Testament prior to that enculturation, in order to enculturate it anew in their own particular milieu. This thesis is not simply false, but it is coarse and lacking in precision. The New Testament was written in Greek and bears the imprint of the Greek spirit, which had already come to maturity as the Old Testament developed. True, there are elements in the evolution of the early Church which do not have to be integrated into all cultures. Nonetheless, the fundamental decisions made about the relationship between faith and the use of human reason are part of the faith itself; they are developments consonant with the nature of faith itself.

And so I come to my conclusion. This attempt, painted with broad strokes, at a critique of modern reason from within has nothing to do with putting the clock back to the time before the Enlightenment and rejecting the insights of the modern age. The positive aspects of modernity are to be acknowledged unreservedly: we are all grateful for the marvelous possibilities that it has opened up for mankind and for the progress in humanity that has been granted to us. The scientific ethos, moreover, is—as you yourself mentioned, Magnificent Rector—the will to be obedient to the truth, and, as such, it embodies an attitude which belongs to the essential decisions of the Christian spirit. The intention here is not one of retrenchment or negative criticism, but of broadening our concept of reason and its application. While we rejoice in the new possibilities open to humanity, we also see the dangers arising from these possibilities and we must ask ourselves how we can overcome them. We will succeed in doing so only if reason and faith come together in a new way, if we overcome the self-imposed limitation of reason to the empirically falsifiable, and if we once more disclose its vast horizons. In this sense theology rightly belongs in the university and within the wide-ranging dialogue of sciences, not merely as a historical discipline and one of the human sciences, but precisely as theology, as inquiry into the rationality of faith.

Only thus do we become capable of that genuine dialogue of cultures and religions so urgently needed today. In the Western world it is widely held that only positivistic reason and the forms of philosophy based on it are universally valid. Yet the world's profoundly religious cultures see this exclusion of the divine from the universality of reason as an attack on their most profound convictions. A reason which is deaf to the divine and which relegates religion into the realm of subcultures is incapable of entering into the dialogue of cultures. At the same time, as I have attempted to show, modern scientific reason with its intrinsically Platonic element bears within itself a question which points beyond itself and beyond the possibilities of its methodology. Modern scientific reason quite simply has to accept the rational structure of matter and the correspondence between our spirit and the prevailing rational structures of nature as a given, on which its methodology has to be based. Yet the question why this has to be so is a real question, and one which has to be remanded by the natural sciences to other modes and planes of thought—to philosophy and theology. For philosophy and, albeit in a different way, for theology, listening to the great experiences and insights of the religious traditions of humanity, and those of the Christian faith in particular, is a source of knowledge, and to ignore it would be an unacceptable restriction of our listening and responding. Here I am reminded of something Socrates said to Phaedo. In their earlier conversations, many false philosophical opinions had been raised, and so Socrates says: "It would be easily understandable if someone became so annoyed at all these false notions that for the rest of his life he despised and mocked all talk about being—but in this way he would be deprived of the truth of existence and would suffer a great loss."[13] The West has long been endangered by this aversion to the questions which underlie its rationality,

---

ologia naturalis, Johannes-Verlag Leutesdorf, 2nd revised edition, 2005.

13 Cf. 90 c-d. For this text, cf. also R. Guardini, *Der Tod des Sokrates*, 5th edition, Mainz-Paderborn 1987, pp. 218–21.

and can only suffer great harm thereby. The courage to engage the whole breadth of reason, and not the denial of its grandeur—this is the program with which a theology grounded in biblical faith enters into the debates of our time. "Not to act reasonably, not to act with *logos*, is contrary to the nature of God," said Manuel II, according to his Christian understanding of God, in response to his Persian interlocutor. It is to this great *logos*, to this breadth of reason, that we invite our partners in the dialogue of cultures. To rediscover it constantly is the great task of the university.

Chapter 4
POPE BENEDICT XVI
Visit to the Bundestag

Reichstag Building, Berlin
September 22, 2011

Mr. President of the Federal Republic,
Mr. President of the Bundestag,
Madam Chancellor,
Madam President of the Bundesrat,
Ladies and Gentlemen Members of the House,

It is an honor and a joy for me to speak before this distinguished house, before the Parliament of my native Germany, that meets here as a democratically elected representation of the people, in order to work for the good of the Federal Republic of Germany. I should like to thank the President of the *Bundestag* both for his invitation to deliver this address and for the kind words of greeting and appreciation with which he has welcomed me. At this moment I turn to you, distinguished ladies and gentlemen, not least as your fellow-countryman who for all his life has been conscious of close links to his origins, and has followed the affairs of his native Germany with keen interest. But the invitation to give this address was extended to me as Pope, as the Bishop of Rome, who bears the highest responsibility for Catholic Christianity. In issuing this invitation you are acknowledging the role that the Holy See plays as a partner within the community of peoples and states. Setting out from this international responsibility that I hold, I should like to propose to you some thoughts on the foundations of a free state of law.

Allow me to begin my reflections on the foundations of law [*Recht*] with a brief story from sacred Scripture. In the First Book of the Kings, it is recounted that God invited the young King Solomon, on his accession to the throne, to make a request. What will the young ruler ask for at this important moment? Success – wealth – long life – destruction of his enemies? He chooses none of these things. Instead, he asks for a listening heart so that he may govern God's people, and discern between good and evil (cf. *1 Kg* 3:9). Through this story, the Bible wants to tell us what should ultimately matter for a politician. His fundamental criterion and the motivation for his work as a politician must not be success, and certainly not material gain. Politics must be a striving for justice, and hence it has to establish the fundamental preconditions for peace. Naturally a politician will seek success, without which he would have no opportunity for effective political action at all. Yet success is subordinated to the criterion of justice, to the will to do what is right, and to the understanding of what is right. Success can also be seductive and thus can open up the path towards the falsification of what is right, towards the destruction of justice. "Without justice—what else is the State but a great band of robbers?", as Saint Augustine once said. We Germans know from our own experience that these words are no empty specter. We have seen how power became divorced from right, how power opposed right and crushed it, so that the State became an instrument for destroying right—a highly organized band of robbers, capable of threatening the whole world and driving it to the edge of the abyss. To serve right and to fight against the dominion of wrong is and remains the fundamental task of the politician. At a moment in history when man has acquired previously inconceivable power, this task takes on a particular urgency. Man can destroy the world. He can manipulate himself. He can, so to speak, make human beings and he can deny them their humanity. How do we recognize what is right? How can we discern between good and evil, between what is truly right and what may appear right? Even now, Solomon's request remains the decisive issue facing politicians and politics today.

For most of the matters that need to be regulated by law, the support of the majority can serve as a sufficient criterion. Yet it is evident that for the fundamental issues of law, in which the dignity of man and of humanity is at stake, the majority principle is not enough: everyone in a position of responsibility must personally seek out the criteria to be followed when framing laws. In the third century, the great theologian Origen provided the following explanation for the resistance of Christians to certain legal systems: "Suppose that a man were living among the Scythians, whose laws are contrary to the divine law, and was compelled to live among them . . . such a man for the sake of the true law, though illegal among the Scythians, would rightly form associations with like-minded people contrary to the laws of the Scythians."[1]

1   *Contra Celsum*, Book 1, Chapter 1. Cf. A. Fürst, "Monotheismus und Monarchie. Zum Zusammenhang von Heil und Herrschaft in der Antike", Theol.Phil. 81 (2006), pp. 321–38,

This conviction was what motivated resistance movements to act against the Nazi regime and other totalitarian regimes, thereby doing a great service to justice and to humanity as a whole. For these people, it was indisputably evident that the law in force was actually unlawful. Yet when it comes to the decisions of a democratic politician, the question of what now corresponds to the law of truth, what is actually right and may be enacted as law, is less obvious. In terms of the underlying anthropological issues, what is right and may be given the force of law is in no way simply self-evident today. The question of how to recognize what is truly right and thus to serve justice when framing laws has never been simple, and today in view of the vast extent of our knowledge and our capacity, it has become still harder.

How do we recognize what is right? In history, systems of law have almost always been based on religion: decisions regarding what was to be lawful among men were taken with reference to the divinity. Unlike other great religions, Christianity has never proposed a revealed law to the State and to society, that is to say a juridical order derived from revelation. Instead, it has pointed to nature and reason as the true sources of law—and to the harmony of objective and subjective reason, which naturally presupposes that both spheres are rooted in the creative reason of God. Christian theologians thereby aligned themselves with a philosophical and juridical movement that began to take shape in the second century B.C. In the first half of that century, the social natural

quoted on p. 336; cf. also J. Ratzinger, Die Einheit der Nationen. Eine Vision der Kirchenväter (Salzburg and Munich, 1971), p. 60.

law developed by the Stoic philosophers came into contact with leading teachers of Roman Law.[2] Through this encounter, the juridical culture of the West was born, which was and is of key significance for the juridical culture of mankind. This pre-Christian marriage between law and philosophy opened up the path that led via the Christian Middle Ages and the juridical developments of the Age of Enlightenment all the way to the *Declaration of Human Rights* and to our German Basic Law of 1949, with which our nation committed itself to "inviolable and inalienable human rights as the foundation of every human community, and of peace and justice in the world."

For the development of law and for the development of humanity, it was highly significant that Christian theologians aligned themselves against the religious law associated with polytheism and on the side of philosophy, and that they acknowledged reason and nature in their interrelation as the universally valid source of law. This step had already been taken by Saint Paul in the Letter to the Romans, when he said: "When Gentiles who have not the Law [the Torah of Israel] do by nature what the law requires, they are a law to themselves . . . they show that what the law requires is written on their hearts, while their conscience also bears witness . . ." (*Rom* 2:14f.). Here we see the two fundamental concepts of nature and conscience, where conscience is nothing other than Solomon's listening heart, reason that is open to the language of being. If this seemed to offer a clear

2 Cf. W. Waldstein, *Ins Herz geschrieben. Das Naturrecht als Fundament einer menschlichen Gesellschaft* (Augsburg, 2010), pp. 11ff., 31–61.

explanation of the foundations of legislation up to the time of the Enlightenment, up to the time of the Declaration on Human Rights after the Second World War and the framing of our Basic Law, there has been a dramatic shift in the situation in the last half-century. The idea of natural law is today viewed as a specifically Catholic doctrine, not worth bringing into the discussion in a non-Catholic environment, so that one feels almost ashamed even to mention the term. Let me outline briefly how this situation arose. Fundamentally it is because of the idea that an unbridgeable gulf exists between "is" and "ought." An "ought" can never follow from an "is," because the two are situated on completely different planes. The reason for this is that in the meantime, the positivist understanding of nature has come to be almost universally accepted. If nature—in the words of Hans Kelsen—is viewed as "an aggregate of objective data linked together in terms of cause and effect," then indeed no ethical indication of any kind can be derived from it.[3] A positivist conception of nature as purely functional, as the natural sciences consider it to be, is incapable of producing any bridge to ethics and law, but once again yields only functional answers. The same also applies to reason, according to the positivist understanding that is widely held to be the only genuinely scientific one. Anything that is not verifiable or falsifiable, according to this understanding, does not belong to the realm of reason strictly understood. Hence ethics and religion must be assigned to the subjective field, and they remain extraneous to the realm of reason in the strict sense of the word. Where positivist reason dominates the field to the

3   Cf. Waldstein, op. cit., pp. 15–21.

exclusion of all else—and that is broadly the case in our public mindset—then the classical sources of knowledge for ethics and law are excluded. This is a dramatic situation which affects everyone, and on which a public debate is necessary. Indeed, an essential goal of this address is to issue an urgent invitation to launch one.

The positivist approach to nature and reason, the positivist world view in general, is a most important dimension of human knowledge and capacity that we may in no way dispense with. But in and of itself it is not a sufficient culture corresponding to the full breadth of the human condition. Where positivist reason considers itself the only sufficient culture and banishes all other cultural realities to the status of subcultures, it diminishes man, indeed it threatens his humanity. I say this with Europe specifically in mind, where there are concerted efforts to recognize only positivism as a common culture and a common basis for law-making, reducing all the other insights and values of our culture to the level of subculture, with the result that Europe vis-à-vis other world cultures is left in a state of culturelessness and at the same time extremist and radical movements emerge to fill the vacuum. In its self-proclaimed exclusivity, the positivist reason which recognizes nothing beyond mere functionality resembles a concrete bunker with no windows, in which we ourselves provide lighting and atmospheric conditions, being no longer willing to obtain either from God's wide world. And yet we cannot hide from ourselves the fact that even in this artificial world, we are still covertly drawing upon God's raw materials, which we refashion into our own products. The windows must be flung open again, we must see the wide world, the sky and the earth once more and learn to make proper use of all this.

But how are we to do this? How do we find our way out into the wide world, into the big picture? How can reason rediscover its true greatness, without being sidetracked into irrationality? How can nature reassert itself in its true depth, with all its demands, with all its directives? I would like to recall one of the developments in recent political history, hoping that I will neither be misunderstood, nor provoke too many one-sided polemics. I would say that the emergence of the ecological movement in German politics since the 1970s, while it has not exactly flung open the windows, nevertheless was and continues to be a cry for fresh air which must not be ignored or pushed aside, just because too much of it is seen to be irrational. Young people had come to realize that something is wrong in our relationship with nature, that matter is not just raw material for us to shape at will, but that the earth has a dignity of its own and that we must follow its directives. In saying this, I am clearly not promoting any particular political party—nothing could be further from my mind. If something is wrong in our relationship with reality, then we must all reflect seriously on the whole situation and we are all prompted to question the very foundations of our culture. Allow me to dwell a little longer on this point. The importance of ecology is no longer disputed. We must listen to the language of nature and we must answer accordingly. Yet I would like to underline a point that seems to me to be neglected, today as in the past: there is also an ecology of man. Man too has a nature that he must respect and that he cannot manipulate at will. Man is not merely self-creating freedom. Man does not create himself. He is intellect and will, but he is also nature, and his will is rightly ordered if he respects his nature, listens to it and accepts himself for who he is, as one who did not create himself. In this way, and in no other, is true human freedom fulfilled.

Let us come back to the fundamental concepts of nature and reason, from which we set out. The great proponent of legal positivism, Kelsen, at the age of 84—in 1965—abandoned the dualism of "is" and "ought." (I find it comforting that rational thought is evidently still possible at the age of 84!) Previously he had said that norms can only come from the will. Nature therefore could only contain norms, he adds, if a will had put them there. But this, he says, would presuppose a Creator God, whose will had entered into nature. "Any attempt to discuss the truth of this belief is utterly futile," he observed.[4] Is it really?—I find myself asking. Is it really pointless to wonder whether the objective reason that manifests itself in nature does not presuppose a creative reason, a *Creator Spiritus*?

At this point Europe's cultural heritage ought to come to our assistance. The conviction that there is a Creator God is what gave rise to the idea of human rights, the idea of the equality of all people before the law, the recognition of the inviolability of human dignity in every single person and the awareness of people's responsibility for their actions. Our cultural memory is shaped by these rational insights. To ignore it or dismiss it as a thing of the past would be to dismember our culture totally and to rob it of its completeness. The culture of Europe arose from the encounter between Jerusalem, Athens and Rome—from the encounter between Israel's monotheism, the philosophical reason of the Greeks and Roman law. This three-way encounter has shaped the

4   Cf. Waldstein, op. cit., p. 19.

inner identity of Europe. In the awareness of man's responsibility before God and in the acknowledgment of the inviolable dignity of every single human person, it has established criteria of law: it is these criteria that we are called to defend at this moment in our history.

As he assumed the mantle of office, the young King Solomon was invited to make a request. How would it be if we, the law-makers of today, were invited to make a request? What would we ask for? I think that, even today, there is ultimately nothing else we could wish for but a listening heart—the capacity to discern between good and evil, and thus to establish true law, to serve justice and peace. I thank you for your attention!

Chapter 5
POPE BENEDICT XVI
Meeting with the Representatives of British Society, including the Diplomatic Corps, Politicians, Academics, and Business Leaders

Westminster Hall - City of Westminster
September 17, 2010

Mr. Speaker,

Thank you for your words of welcome on behalf of this distinguished gathering. As I address you, I am conscious of the privilege afforded me to speak to the British people and their representatives in Westminster Hall, a building of unique significance in the civil and political history of the people of these islands. Allow me also to express my esteem for the Parliament which has existed on this site for centuries and which has had such a profound influence on the development of participative government among the nations, especially in the Commonwealth and the English-speaking world at large. Your common law tradition serves as the basis of legal systems in many parts of the world, and your particular vision of the respective rights and duties of the state and the individual, and of the separation of powers, remains an inspiration to many across the globe.

As I speak to you in this historic setting, I think of the countless men and women down the centuries who have played their part in the momentous events that have taken place within these walls and have shaped the lives of many generations of Britons, and others besides. In particular, I recall the figure of Saint Thomas More, the great English scholar and statesman, who is admired by believers and non-believers alike for the integrity with which he followed his conscience, even at the cost of displeasing the sovereign whose "good servant" he was, because he chose to serve God first. The dilemma which faced More in those difficult times, the perennial question of the relationship between what is owed to Caesar and what is owed to God, allows me the opportunity to reflect with you briefly on the proper place of religious belief within the political process.

This country's Parliamentary tradition owes much to the national instinct for moderation, to the desire to achieve a genuine balance between the legitimate claims of government and the rights of those subject to it. While decisive steps have been taken at several points in your history to place limits on the exercise of power, the nation's political institutions have been able to evolve with a remarkable degree of stability. In the process, Britain has emerged as a pluralist democracy which places great value on freedom of speech, freedom of political affiliation and respect for the rule of law, with a strong sense of the individual's rights and duties, and of the equality of all citizens before the law. While couched in different language, Catholic social teaching has much in common with this approach, in its overriding concern to safeguard the unique dignity of every human person, created in the image and likeness of God, and in its emphasis on the duty of civil authority to foster the common good.

And yet the fundamental questions at stake in Thomas More's trial continue to present themselves in ever-changing terms as new social conditions emerge. Each generation, as it seeks to advance the common good, must ask anew: what are the requirements that governments may reasonably impose upon citizens, and how far do they extend? By appeal to what authority can moral dilemmas be resolved? These questions take us directly to the ethical foundations of civil discourse. If the moral principles underpinning the democratic process are themselves determined by nothing more solid than social consensus, then the fragility of the process becomes all too evident—herein lies the real challenge for democracy.

The inadequacy of pragmatic, short-term solutions to complex social and ethical problems has been illustrated all too clearly by the recent global financial crisis. There is widespread agreement that the lack of a solid ethical foundation for economic activity has contributed to the grave difficulties now being experienced by millions of people throughout the world. Just as "every economic decision has a moral consequence" (*Caritas in Veritate*, 37), so too in the political field, the ethical dimension of policy has far-reaching consequences that no government can afford to ignore. A positive illustration of this is found in one of the British Parliament's particularly notable achievements—the abolition of the slave trade. The campaign that led to this landmark legislation was built upon firm ethical principles, rooted in the natural law, and it has made a contribution to civilization of which this nation may be justly proud.

The central question at issue, then, is this: where is the ethical foundation for political choices to be found? The Catholic tradition maintains that the objective norms governing right action are accessible to reason, prescinding from the content of revelation. According to this understanding, the role of religion in political debate is not so much to supply these norms, as if they could not be known by non-believers—still less to propose concrete political solutions, which would lie altogether outside the competence of religion—but rather to help purify and shed light upon the application of reason to the discovery of objective moral principles. This "corrective" role of religion vis-à-vis reason is not always welcomed, though, partly because distorted forms of religion, such as sectarianism and fundamentalism, can be seen to create serious social problems themselves. And in their turn, these distortions of religion arise when insufficient attention is given to the purifying and structuring role of reason within religion. It is a two-way process. Without the corrective supplied by religion, though, reason too can fall prey to distortions, as when it is manipulated by ideology, or applied in a partial way that fails to take full account of the dignity of the human person. Such misuse of reason, after all, was what gave rise to the slave trade in the first place and to many other social evils, not least the totalitarian ideologies of the twentieth century. This is why I would suggest that the world of reason and the world of faith—the world of secular rationality and the world of religious belief—need one another and should not be afraid to enter into a profound and ongoing dialogue, for the good of our civilization.

Religion, in other words, is not a problem for legislators to solve, but a vital contributor to the national conversation.

Chapter 5

In this light, I cannot but voice my concern at the increasing marginalization of religion, particularly of Christianity, that is taking place in some quarters, even in nations which place a great emphasis on tolerance. There are those who would advocate that the voice of religion be silenced, or at least relegated to the purely private sphere. There are those who argue that the public celebration of festivals such as Christmas should be discouraged, in the questionable belief that it might somehow offend those of other religions or none. And there are those who argue—paradoxically with the intention of eliminating discrimination—that Christians in public roles should be required at times to act against their conscience. These are worrying signs of a failure to appreciate not only the rights of believers to freedom of conscience and freedom of religion, but also the legitimate role of religion in the public square. I would invite all of you, therefore, within your respective spheres of influence, to seek ways of promoting and encouraging dialogue between faith and reason at every level of national life.

Your readiness to do so is already implied in the unprecedented invitation extended to me today. And it finds expression in the fields of concern in which your Government has been engaged with the Holy See. In the area of peace, there have been exchanges regarding the elaboration of an international arms trade treaty; regarding human rights, the Holy See and the United Kingdom have welcomed the spread of democracy, especially in the last sixty-five years; in the field of development, there has been collaboration on debt relief, fair trade and financing for development, particularly through the International Finance Facility, the International Immunization Bond, and the Advanced Market Commitment. The Holy See also looks forward to exploring with the United Kingdom new ways to promote environmental responsibility, to the benefit of all.

I also note that the present Government has committed the United Kingdom to devoting 0.7% of national income to development aid by 2013. In recent years it has been encouraging to witness the positive signs of a worldwide growth in solidarity towards the poor. But to turn this solidarity into effective action calls for fresh thinking that will improve life conditions in many important areas, such as food production, clean water, job creation, education, support to families, especially migrants, and basic healthcare. Where human lives are concerned, time is always short: yet the world has witnessed the vast resources that governments can draw upon to rescue financial institutions deemed "too big to fail." Surely the integral human development of the world's peoples is no less important: here is an enterprise, worthy of the world's attention, that is truly "too big to fail."

This overview of recent cooperation between the United Kingdom and the Holy See illustrates well how much progress has been made, in the years that have passed since the establishment of bilateral diplomatic relations, in promoting throughout the world the many core values that we share. I hope and pray that this relationship will continue to bear fruit, and that it will be mirrored in a growing acceptance of the need for dialogue and respect at every level of society between the world of reason and the world of faith. I am convinced that, within this country too, there are many areas in which the Church and the public authorities can work together for the good of citizens, in harmony with this Parliament's historic practice of invoking the Spirit's guidance upon those who seek to improve the conditions of all mankind. For such cooperation to be possible, religious bodies—including institutions linked to the Catholic Church—need to be free to act in accordance with their own principles and specific convictions based upon the faith and the official teaching of the Church. In this way, such basic rights as religious freedom, freedom of conscience and freedom of association are guaranteed. The angels looking down on us from the magnificent ceiling of this ancient Hall remind us of the long tradition from which British Parliamentary democracy has evolved. They remind us that God is constantly watching over us to guide and protect us. And they summon us to acknowledge the vital contribution that religious belief has made and can continue to make to the life of the nation.

Mr. Speaker, I thank you once again for this opportunity briefly to address this distinguished audience. Let me assure you and the Lord Speaker of my continued good wishes and prayers for you and for the fruitful work of both Houses of this ancient Parliament. Thank you and God bless you all!

Chapter 6
POPE BENEDICT XVI
Ecumenical Meeting

Throne Hall of the Archbishop's House of Prague
September 27, 2009

Dear Cardinals,
Your Excellencies,
Brothers and Sisters in Christ,

I am grateful to Almighty God for the opportunity to meet with you who are here representing the various Christian communities of this land. I thank Doctor Cerný, President of the Ecumenical Council of Churches in the Czech Republic, for the kind words of welcome which he has addressed to me on your behalf.

My dear friends, Europe continues to undergo many changes. It is hard to believe that only two decades have passed since the collapse of former regimes gave way to a difficult but productive transition towards more participatory political structures. During this period, Christians joined together with others of good will in helping to rebuild a just political order, and they continue to engage in dialogue today in order to pave new ways towards mutual understanding, cooperation for peace and the advancement of the common good.

Nevertheless, attempts to marginalize the influence of Christianity upon public life—sometimes under the pretext that its teachings are detrimental to the well-being of society—are emerging in new forms. This phenomenon gives us pause to reflect. As I suggested in my Encyclical on Christian hope, the artificial separation of the Gospel from intellectual and public life should prompt us to engage in a mutual "self-critique of modernity" and "self-critique of modern Christianity," specifically with regard to the hope each of them can offer mankind (cf. *Spe Salvi*, 22). We may ask ourselves, what does the Gospel have to say to the Czech Republic and indeed all of Europe today in a period marked by proliferating world views?

Christianity has much to offer on the practical and ethical level, for the Gospel never ceases to inspire men and women to place themselves at the service of their brothers and sisters. Few would dispute this. Yet those who fix their gaze upon Jesus of Nazareth with eyes of faith know that God offers a deeper reality which is nonetheless inseparable from the "economy" of charity at work in this world (cf. *Caritas in Veritate*, 2): He offers *salvation*.

The term is replete with connotations, yet it expresses something fundamental and universal about the human yearning for well-being and wholeness. It alludes to the ardent desire for reconciliation and communion that wells up spontaneously in the depths of the human spirit. It is the central truth of the Gospel and the goal to which every effort of evangelization and pastoral care is directed. And it is the criterion to which Christians constantly redirect their focus as they endeavor to heal the wounds of past divisions. To this end—as Doctor Cerný has noted—the Holy See was pleased to host an International Symposium in 1999 on Jan Hus to facilitate a discussion of the complex and turbulent religious history in this country and in Europe more generally (cf. Pope John Paul II, *Address to the International Symposium on John Hus,* 1999). I pray that such ecumenical initiatives will yield fruit not only in the pursuit of Christian unity, but for the good of all European society.

We take confidence in knowing that the Church's proclamation of salvation in Christ Jesus is ever ancient and ever new, steeped in the wisdom of the past and brimming with hope for the future. As Europe listens to the story of Christianity, she hears her own. Her notions of justice, freedom and social responsibility, together with the cultural and legal institutions established to preserve these ideas and hand them on to future generations, are shaped by her Christian inheritance. Indeed, her memory of the past animates her aspirations for the future.

This is why, in fact, Christians draw upon the example of figures such as Saint Adalbert and Saint Agnes of Bohemia. Their commitment to spreading the Gospel was motivated by the conviction that Christians should not cower in fear of the world but rather confidently share the treasury of truths entrusted to them. Likewise Christians today, opening themselves to present realities and affirming all that is good in society, must have the courage to invite men and women to the radical conversion that ensues upon an encounter with Christ and ushers in a new life of grace.

From this perspective, we understand more clearly why Christians are obliged to join others in reminding Europe of her roots. It is not because these roots have long since withered. On the contrary! It is because they continue—in subtle but nonetheless fruitful ways—to supply the continent with the spiritual and moral sustenance that allows her to enter into meaningful dialogue with people from other cultures and religions. Precisely because the Gospel is not an ideology, it does not presume to lock evolving socio-political realities into rigid schemas. Rather, it transcends the vicissitudes of this world and casts new light on the dignity of the human person in every age. Dear friends, let us ask the Lord to implant within us a spirit of courage to share the timeless saving truths which have shaped, and will continue to shape, the social and cultural progress of this continent.

The salvation wrought by Jesus' suffering, death, resurrection and ascension into heaven not only transforms us who believe in him, but urges us to share this Good News with others. Enlightened by the Spirit's gifts of knowledge, wisdom and understanding (cf. *Is.* 11:1-2; *Ex.* 35:31), may our capacity to grasp the truth taught by Jesus Christ impel us to work tirelessly for the unity he desires for all his children reborn through Baptism, and indeed for the whole human race.

With these sentiments, and with fraternal affection for you and the members of your respective communities, I express my deep thanks to you and commend you to Almighty God, who is our fortress, our stronghold and our deliverer (cf. *Ps.* 144:2). Amen.

Appendix

On April 18, 2005, then-Cardinal Joseph Ratzinger gave a memorable homily to the conclave that would soon elect him as the successor of Pope John Paul II. Cardinal Ratzinger concluded that homily praying that God "will once again give us a Pastor according to his own heart, a Pastor who will guide us to knowledge of Christ, to his love and to true joy." The homily, however, grabbed headlines for the Cardinal's powerful and eloquent warning about the dangers of the contemporary drift, predominantly in the West, toward "a dictatorship of relativism." While many people know of the homily due to that remark, comparatively few people have actually read the complete homily. The homily is reproduced here in full.

CARDINAL JOSEPH RATZINGER

Mass Pro Eligendo Romano Pontifice

Vatican Basilica, April 18, 2005

At this moment of great responsibility, let us listen with special attention to what the Lord says to us in his own words. I would like to examine just a few passages from the three readings that concern us directly at this time.

The first one offers us a prophetic portrait of the person of the Messiah— a portrait that receives its full meaning from the moment when Jesus reads the text in the synagogue at Nazareth and says, "Today this Scripture passage is fulfilled in your hearing" (Lk 4: 21).

At the core of the prophetic text we find a word which seems contradictory, at least at first sight. The Messiah, speaking of himself, says that he was sent "to announce a year of favor from the Lord and a day of vindication by our God" (Is 61: 2). We hear with joy the news of a year of favor: divine mercy puts a limit on evil, as the Holy Father told us. Jesus Christ is divine mercy in person: encountering Christ means encountering God's mercy.

Christ's mandate has become our mandate through the priestly anointing. We are called to proclaim, not only with our words but also with our lives and with the valuable signs of the sacraments, "the year of favor from the Lord."

But what does the prophet Isaiah mean when he announces "the day of vindication by our God"? At Nazareth, Jesus omitted these words in his reading of the prophet's text; he concluded by announcing the year of favor. Might this have been the reason for the outburst of scandal after his preaching? We do not know.

In any case, the Lord offered a genuine commentary on these words by being put to death on the cross. St. Peter says: "In his own body he brought your sins to the cross" (I Pt 2: 24). And St. Paul writes in his Letter to the Galatians: "Christ has delivered us from the power of the law's curse by himself becoming a curse for us, as it is written, 'Accursed is anyone who is hanged on a tree.' This happened so that through Christ Jesus the blessing bestowed on Abraham might descend on the Gentiles in Christ Jesus, thereby making it possible for us to receive the promised Spirit through faith" (Gal 3: 13f.).

Christ's mercy is not a grace that comes cheap, nor does it imply the trivialization of evil. Christ carries the full weight of evil and all its destructive force in his body and in his soul. He burns and transforms evil in suffering, in the fire of his suffering love. The day of vindication and the year of favor converge in the Paschal Mystery, in the dead and Risen Christ. This is the vengeance of God: he himself suffers for us, in the person of his Son. The more deeply stirred we are by the Lord's mercy, the greater the solidarity we feel with his suffering—and we become willing to complete in our own flesh "what is lacking in the afflictions of Christ" (Col 1: 24).

Let us move on to the second reading, the letter to the Ephesians. Here we see essentially three aspects: first of all, the ministries and charisms in the Church as gifts of the Lord who rose and ascended into heaven; then, the maturing of faith and the knowledge of the Son of God as the condition and content of unity in the Body of Christ; and lastly, our common participation in the growth of the Body of Christ, that is, the transformation of the world into communion with the Lord.

Let us dwell on only two points. The first is the journey towards "the maturity of Christ," as the Italian text says, simplifying it slightly. More precisely, in accordance with the Greek text, we should speak of the "measure of the fullness of Christ" that we are called to attain if we are to be true adults in the faith. We must not remain children in faith, in the condition of minors. And what does it mean to be children in faith? St. Paul answers: it means being "tossed here and there, carried about by every wind of doctrine" (Eph 4: 14). This description is very timely!

How many winds of doctrine have we known in recent decades, how many ideological currents, how many ways of thinking. The small boat of the thought of many Christians has often been tossed about by these waves—flung from one extreme to another: from Marxism to liberalism, even to libertinism; from collectivism to radical individualism; from atheism to a vague religious mysticism; from agnosticism to syncretism and so forth. Every day new sects spring up, and what St. Paul says about human deception and the trickery that strives to entice people into error (cf. Eph 4: 14) comes true.

Today, having a clear faith based on the Creed of the Church is often labeled as fundamentalism. Whereas relativism, that is, letting oneself be "tossed here and there, carried about by every wind of doctrine," seems the only attitude that can cope with modern times. We are building a dictatorship of relativism that does not recognize anything as definitive and whose ultimate goal consists solely of one's own ego and desires.

We, however, have a different goal: the Son of God, the true man. He is the measure of true humanism. An "adult" faith is not a faith that follows the trends of fashion and the latest novelty; a mature adult faith is deeply rooted in friendship with Christ. It is this friendship that opens us up to all that is good and gives us a criterion by which to distinguish the true from the false, and deceit from truth.

We must develop this adult faith; we must guide the flock of Christ to this faith. And it is this faith—only faith—that creates unity and is fulfilled in love.

On this theme, St. Paul offers us as a fundamental formula for Christian existence some beautiful words, in contrast to the continual vicissitudes of those who, like children, are tossed about by the waves: make truth in love. Truth and love coincide in Christ. To the extent that we draw close to Christ, in our own lives too, truth and love are blended. Love without truth would be blind; truth without love would be like "a clanging cymbal" (I Cor 13: 1).

Let us now look at the Gospel, from whose riches I would like to draw only two small observations. The Lord addresses these wonderful words to us: "I no longer speak of you as slaves. . . . Instead, I call you friends" (Jn 15: 15). We so often feel, and it is true, that we are only useless servants (cf. Lk 17: 10).

Yet, in spite of this, the Lord calls us friends, he makes us his friends, he gives us his friendship. The Lord gives friendship a dual definition. There are no secrets between friends: Christ tells us all that he hears from the Father; he gives us his full trust and with trust, also knowledge. He reveals his face and his heart to us. He shows us the tenderness he feels for us, his passionate love that goes even as far as the folly of the Cross. He entrusts himself to us, he gives us the power to speak in his name: "this is my body . . . ," "I forgive you . . . ." He entrusts his Body, the Church, to us.

To our weak minds, to our weak hands, he entrusts his truth—the mystery of God the Father, the Son and the Holy Spirit; the mystery of God who "so loved the world that he gave his only Son" (Jn 3: 16). He made us his friends—and how do we respond?

The second element Jesus uses to define friendship is the communion of wills. For the Romans *"Idem velle—idem nolle"* [same desires, same dislikes] was also the definition of friendship. "You are my friends if you do what I command you" (Jn 15: 14). Friendship with Christ coincides with the third request of the *Our Father:* "Thy will be done on earth as it is in heaven." At his hour in the Garden of Gethsemane, Jesus transformed our rebellious human will into a will conformed and united with the divine will. He suffered the whole drama of our autonomy—and precisely by placing our will in God's hands, he gives us true freedom: "Not as I will, but as you will" (Mt 26: 39).

Our redemption is brought about in this communion of wills: being friends of Jesus, to become friends of God. The more we love Jesus, the more we know him, the more our true freedom develops and our joy in being redeemed flourishes. Thank you, Jesus, for your friendship!

The other element of the Gospel to which I wanted to refer is Jesus's teaching on bearing fruit: "It was I who chose you to go forth and bear fruit. Your fruit must endure" (Jn 15: 16).

It is here that appears the dynamism of the life of a Christian, an apostle: *I chose you to go forth.* We must be enlivened by a holy restlessness: a restlessness to bring to everyone the gift of faith, of friendship with Christ. Truly, the love and friendship of God was given to us so that it might also be shared with others. We have received the faith to give it to others—we are priests in order to serve others. And we must bear fruit that will endure.

All people desire to leave a lasting mark. But what endures? Money does not. Even buildings do not, nor books. After a certain time, longer or shorter, all these things disappear. The only thing that lasts forever is the human soul, the human person created by God for eternity.

The fruit that endures is therefore all that we have sown

in human souls: love, knowledge, a gesture capable of touching hearts, words that open the soul to joy in the Lord. So let us go and pray to the Lord to help us bear fruit that endures. Only in this way will the earth be changed from a valley of tears to a garden of God.

To conclude, let us return once again to the Letter to the Ephesians. The Letter says, with words from *Psalm 68*, that Christ, ascending into heaven, "gave gifts to men" (Eph 4: 8). The victor offers gifts. And these gifts are apostles, prophets, evangelists, pastors and teachers. Our ministry is a gift of Christ to humankind, to build up his body—the new world. We live out our ministry in this way, as a gift of Christ to humanity!

At this time, however, let us above all pray insistently to the Lord that after his great gift of Pope John Paul II, he will once again give us a Pastor according to his own heart, a Pastor who will guide us to knowledge of Christ, to his love and to true joy. Amen.

Marc D. Guerra, Ph.D., is associate professor and chair of the Department of Theology at Assumption College. He has published *Christians as Political Animals: Taking the Measure of Modernity and Modern Democracy* and *Reason, Revelation and Human Affairs*. Guerra's edited volumes include *Jerusalem, Athens, and Rome: Essays in Honor of James V. Schall, s.j., Pope Benedict XVI and the Politics of Modernity*, and, with Peter Augustine Lawler, *The Science of Modern Virtue: Essays on Descartes, Locke, and Darwin*.

James V. Schall. s.j., retired from his post as a professor of political philosophy in the Department of Government at Georgetown University in 2012. He is the author of hundreds of essays on political, theological, literary, and philosophical questions and themes. Schall's numerous books include *The Regensburg Lecture, At the Limits of Political Philosophy, The Mind That Is Catholic, Jacques Maritain: The Philosopher in Society, On the Unseriousness of Human Affairs, Roman Catholic Political Philosophy, Schall on Chesterton*, and *The Modern Age*.